To my family and friends who stuck by my side through my darkest days. **I love you to the moon and back.**

I've changed your names for confidentiality. But, you know who you are.

May this book explain the depths of an eating disorder (ED) struggle and save someone's life (and the lives of his or her family) before it's too late. Seven million women and one million men suffer from an ED. That number is ever increasing. Eating disorders have the highest mortality rate of any mental illness. The pandemic has to stop.

*Please note: Eating Disorder will be referred to as ED numerous times throughout this book. It's the accepted label at Remuda Ranch, basically personified as the devil, who has no right to be in anyone's life.

September, 2010

Meg,

I love you so much and will fight for you until the end. Just never give up on yourself, no matter who is there or what happens. Always believe in yourself. You will beat this.
Love,
John

A note left on my laptop the morning after a breakdown. I had hit rock bottom. Crying and crying, driving around and not answering my phone, and causing panic for my loved ones. I went to John's house, my boyfriend of one year, and cried in his arms. I was broken. I couldn't live like this anymore. I was never thin enough, never good enough, always on the go and always scrounging to keep busy, to keep my mind off of food until I became ravishingly hungry. Once I hit the ravishing point, I gave in and binged. Though a binge, in my eyes, was not merely enough for a marathon runner's entire daily intake, the guilt would claw me like a monster and my finger would reach for my throat, an instinct of self-discipline. I didn't deserve the pleasure of food. My body didn't deserve nourishment. So, I purged. I cleansed until I was empty. Empty of emotion and numbed with swollen glands, a sore throat and blood shot eyes.

Sitting on the ground of John's room, folding his laundry and trying to calm down, we began to talk about the inevitable. Why did I think I was fat? Why was I so upset? What had triggered this? What was going on? I didn't even know. My brain was so far gone, so encroached in the image of an eating disorder, a habitual cycle of hell; I was losing my best friend, my boyfriend, my soul mate, the man I wanted to marry one day. The core of most of our arguments, my insecurity, low self-esteem and hatred of my body was creeping into the middle of two souls meant for one another.

Before Treatment
March, 2005

Today, I hung out with my roommate and noticed some strange behaviors. I'm not exactly the inquisitive type; you could change the color of my bedroom walls and I may not take a second glance. But, for some reason, I was a little taken aback with Jessica's actions. I never really thought much of it, as a track and cross-country athlete, I was always at practice, class, or eating meals with the team. You could find me studying at the library most nights, with my designated cubicle where I'd tally the hours I'd spent studying.

When I headed back to the dorm room, it was usually only for a few minutes, to take a shower, get changed or check a few e-mails. It became a theme that whenever I came back to the room, Jessica had just finished working out at the student fitness center. In her cut-off t-shirts and baggy red gym shorts, she looked frail. I didn't think much of it. She was naturally thin, just like me, and I guess she just liked to burn off some steam doing the elliptical for hours at a time.

Sometimes the bathroom door would be shut for hours at a time. I guess she liked to take long showers. Little did I know, she was likely in there purging. Getting rid of any little calories that still existed in her body. She was obsessing about her thighs, her arms and stomach, pinching the skin and wishing it would all just disappear. Stashed in her shelves were low-fat cereals and half –eaten low-calorie cereal bars. That was it.

April, 2005

I ate a little too much. I was visiting the girls down the hallway, watching *Sex in the City* and decided to partake in the ice cream festivities. We walked down to United Dairy Farmer's (UDF) and carefully selected the gooey, tasty half pint cartons of Ben &Jerry's ice cream, to eat to our heart's content. I chose Fish Food, consisting of solid chocolate fish encased in vanilla bean ice cream, with caramel and dark chocolate swirls. We went back to the dorm room, popped on the television and began indulging, all the while gossiping about the latest trends, laughing about the drunken festivities of the weekend, and procrastinating until the wee hours of the evening to do our dreaded assignments.

As I walked down the hall to my room, to grab my 30-pound book bag, and commence my trek to the dreaded library cubicle, I felt overly full. Maybe I should get rid of the caloric glob of melted dairy product in my belly. It didn't feel so good. Yes, just this once, I could try to make it come up. I hunched over the toilet, stuck my finger down my throat and watched as the milky substance soon filled the toilet. That was easy.

May, 2005

I'm not quite thin enough. I'm going to keep a food diary and running log this summer. It will be my last season to make my goals in cross-country. I was the most valuable runner my sophomore year, but nothing my junior year. Maybe if I lost 10-15 pounds, I could be fast again. It seems like all the really fast girls – the ones who qualify for Nationals consecutively- are skin and bones. They have less to carry. I need less to carry.

June 1, 2005

Weight: ___ (this is when I began obsessing over the scale. I would weight myself at least five times per day).

Miles run: 7
Felt crummy. I had side cramps and could hardly breathe. Thank gosh for the Justin Timberlake

soundtrack, or I probably would have quite around mile 2.

Breakfast: None (yay!)

Lunch: 2 GIANT bowls of Kashi cereal. I was really hungry after my run. I kept telling myself that I could stave off until dinner, but I gave in. (bad!)

Dinner: Grilled cheese and tomato soup
Snack: Yogurt, a handful of peanuts

June 15, 2005

Weight: ___

Miles run: 9
Felt great! I went to the park and did the loop three times. The weather was perfect, the trees were beautiful and I got lost in the moment. It's runs like these that remind me why I run in the first place.

Breakfast: Toast with 5 calorie spray butter

Lunch: Nada! I had such a high from my run, that I simply wasn't interested in "food".

Dinner: Mom's macaroni and cheese. Heavenly delicious, but sinfully caloric. MUST RUN MORE. MUST EAT LESS.

July 8, 2005

Weight: ___

Miles run: 4
Feeling extra fat. With a side of fat.

Breakfast: Cinnamon Toast Crunch

Lunch: 2 Slices of Papa John's Pizza

Dinner: BLT sandwich and side salad

Wow. I need to slim down. Hopefully cross-country camp will get me back in shape. We have two-per-day runs, and lately, I don't like eating in front of others, so perhaps this will be the secret to my success.

Digging Deeper

I wish I would have stopped there. With eating disorders, the earlier you catch them, the higher the chance that you'll recover and move on with your life. If you can "nip it in the bud," and get help early on, confide in someone to talk to about how you're feeling, how thoughts calories and exercise seems to take up 95% of your brain activity, you have a better shot of escaping the miserable cycle. I just want other young girls to feel open and comfortable about talking and asking for help. It can save us from this increasing epidemic; I just know it. If I could have done one thing differently, I would have opened up about my strange obsession, and saved myself from wasting seven years of my life suffocated with hateful, self-destructive thoughts and behaviors.

Unfortunately, I ignored the signs and kept moving deeper and deeper until I had a full-fledged eating disorder by my second semester of my senior year at college.

One of my best friends and college teammate's, Fannie, confessed to me late one night that she had been struggling with an eating disorder since the age of 12. I was so mad at myself for missing the signs. She used to eat, quite a bit, and even became champion of the food hall in eating contests against the boy runners, but I ignorantly thought it was just because she ran and burned it, her body needed extra fuel. She used to ask me, day after day, if she looked "fatter," and vent about how she hated her body. I didn't think much of it. I figured she was a girl, just like me, who had some self-esteem things going on because of outside circumstances. We were, after all, usually surrounded by stick-thin girls, racing in buns (glorified underwear that oftentimes made you think you were running naked), and comparing our times, our techniques, and our *bodies* every day of our collegiate career.

If Fannie was bulimic, getting rid of all the food that went into her small body, perhaps I should go back to those habits I began to fall into last summer. The devil in my head was striking back and hard this time. Fannie was our number one runner on the varsity cross-country, indoor and outdoor teams. I always thought she was just a natural, and I'm sure genetics did assist with her extreme talent, but if bulimia was working for her, I bet it could work for me, too. That night, I decided not to eat. That next day, I decided not to eat. That night, I binged on flour and sugar (the only thing my roommate had in the cupboard, as I tried not to keep food around much anymore), and puked until I was completely empty. Empty of feeling. I didn't feel like the inadequate, slow runner that I believed myself to be. I deserved to be punished. I didn't deserve to eat. After all, all these years, all these girls who were beating me across the finish line, they weren't indulging in meals and letting their bodies soak in the caloric mess; they were smarter. My body deserved pay-back.

Summer 2006

I graduated. Woopity-doo. Now, it was time to figure out what I wanted to do with the rest of my life, and put all those tuition dollars to work

Everyone seemed to already have their bachelor degree plus five-years of work-experience, so I felt behind from the start. I decided to re-enroll in school, this time earning a master's degree in communications management with a concentration on public relations. I started the program in community counseling, originally, and switched after one semester, realizing it wasn't the program for me. Decision-making was never a strong point of mine, and I was easily influenced by other's opinions; a trait, which I later realized, was common among those with eating disorders. I wanted to please others, put others first, and I sacrificed my own well-being for this. I didn't learn to have a backbone until years later.

That first summer post-undergrad was a tough one. I moved back home, didn't have the safety and tight network of college friends constantly surrounding me, and didn't feel like the honorable Dean's List All-Academic athlete title earned in college meant anything in the real world. There was lots of competition out there. I was just a meandering girl on the verge of anorexia. I worked at a publishing company, one where I had interned the summer before, and began turning to restricting like never before. The shaky high that came from three days of restricting gave me something no one else could have. I was in control. For breakfast, one cup of dry apple cinnamon cheerios, secured in a tight Ziploc baggy and nibbled throughout the morning, along with a coffee and one teaspoon on non-fat, no-sugar French vanilla creamer. For lunch, one apple and two plain rice cakes. A glass of water to wash it down. For dinner, it depended heavily. Usually I got away with some cereal and a yogurt. Sometimes, when mom and dad were there, I ate what they ate, though mainly pushed it around on my plate, played with it until it looked sufficiently eaten and poured it down the garbage disposal when no one was looking.

My weight began to plummet quite quickly, at first. I began popping laxatives to rid my body of the small amount of food I did ingest. I went to body sculpting classes with mom twice a week, took the stairs to the fifth floor every morning, snuck in miles before and after work (when I didn't have silly graduate night classes to interfere with my regimen), did 100 sit ups before bed every night and stuck to my cereal, apple and rice cake diet. By the end of the summer, I was down to 113 pounds. It still sounded fat to me, but I was 5' 9". I wanted to strive for double-digits. Nothing was enough, and nothing would EVER be enough for ED. For years to come, ED was never pleased, no matter what the scale said.

I worked and went to graduate school, stayed busy so I simply didn't have time to eat. I remember one night when mom sat next to me on the basement stairs, asking what was wrong. She said I looked too skinny. I said she was wrong. I ignored it and kept going, going, going, joined a gym and starting working at a running store on the side, where my habits were reinforced by the other skinny athletes. My size two pants were baggy on my skeletal legs. My size zero pants weren't fitting anymore, either. It was liberating. I was in control.

I kept up with this behavior for about a year. Restricting and running. My body became used to it. In fact, I began training for my first marathon, which later became an unhealthy addiction, and ran it in 3 hours and 19 minutes. I used long training runs as an excuse to go run for two hours, on a regular basis. My body put up with it. Thank God. Sometimes I seriously wonder how. Eventually, though, my body wanted to binge.

June 2007

Fannie and I went to Colorado to visit our friend Ken. We were so excited and giddy to get away for a few days and take our first real "post-grad" trip – to Denver, none the less! A cool, hipster area, Ken would show us around, we'd drink mojitos on the rooftop bars, go swimming in the river, lay out by the pool and tour the Coor's Light facility.

I met Fannie at the airport, excited as can be. I hadn't seen her in three or four months, which was far too long to be separated from my partner in crime. She told me I looked like a skeleton. "I can see every bone in your back through that tank top," she said. Whatever! Who is she kidding, I thought?

We checked-in, found security and went to our gate. "Are you hungry?" she asked. No, I said. I used the continual excuse: I already ate! So, we skipped the food and went to our gate, painting our nails hot pink and giggling about all the trouble we got in during college. This was going to be a great trip, I just knew it.

When we finally arrived to Denver, I was happy as a lark, able to sustain my hunger and survive with a hot cinnamon tea and splenda from Starbucks. Ken was there, bright eyed and smiling, just how I remembered him. We went to his townhouse, sat on the balcony and started drinking! One drink later and I was a little woozy; the altitude caught me off guard. Apparently, one drink in Denver was equivalent to three drinks in Ohio (or something like that). We had such fun that night, creating our own liquor-infused concoction, which we so creatively named "The Denver". Strawberry schnapps, which tasted like jolly ranchers, mixed with some Sprite; needless to say, without any food for the duration of the day, "The Denver" went straight to my head. That night I slept out on the couch and coaxed myself to sleep, hushing my grumbling belly and reminding myself how I had to wear my Victoria's Secret bikini tomorrow. I couldn't have a bulge in my stomach. The cellulite on my thighs needed to starve. So, I drank some water and soon fell asleep. Looking back, I'm amazed how my heart put up with this. I'm thankful that my body adjusted to this kind of treatment, though it never deserved to go through that. At the time, starving was self-satisfying. If I couldn't be the smartest, the happiest, the most successful or the funniest, at least I could strive to be the thinnest. Right?

The next morning, I went to get a coffee mug from the cupboard. I fainted and hit my head on the cabinet, then on the floor. Ken and Fannie came rushing to the kitchen, hearing the big bang of my body hitting the ceramic tile. I jumped up like a deer in headlights and told them I accidentally tripped. My body was telling me to eat. My head was telling me that I didn't deserve it. Throughout the trip, I nibbled on oatmeal and tortilla chips, staving off the hunger and allowing myself to indulge in a few drinks in the evening. I found that mojitos had 100 calories, so I mostly stuck with that. I remember eating at a sub place one evening, nibbling on the corner of the bread and telling myself I was full, as the others ate collectively and calmly. I no longer knew how to do that; it was either all or nothing. When I ate, which was few and far between, I *ate* quickly and manically, until my stomach was full beyond reason. Those days were followed by either days of restricting, over-exercising, throwing up or using laxatives. Mostly, though, at this point in the disorder, I chose to starve. After Fannie ate, seemingly cool and collective, she and I went to the ladies' room where she proceeded to throw up and complain how only the lettuce was coming up.

In July, my oldest sister, Diane, got married. Looking back at the pictures, I looked unhealthy, skeletal, really. At the time, I saw myself as obese. Some days, I still see myself as obese, but my wise mind and strength to see outside of ED's eyes doesn't obsess like I did then. Any event involving food scared me half to death. I'd avoid them like the plague. I skipped friend's bachelorette parties, wedding showers and social gatherings, just so I wasn't setting myself up for interrogation or failure. The thought of those situations made me sweat and shake. My sister's wedding, though, I could not skip. I got up early to get my five mile run in and punished myself for indulging in a side of pasta at the rehearsal dinner. I got through lunch at the church without swallowing a single bite and I nibbled on some lettuce at the dinner. I remember being lightheaded during my maid-of-honor speech, praying I didn't fall and make a scene at my sister's special day, which was only to celebrate love and happiness. I drank some wine and too much vodka. I missed half the reception and passed out in the upstairs of the venue. I had to be carried out. I was mortified. My body couldn't handle alcohol very well to begin with, and once I turned anorexic, my body reacted quite quickly. My eating disorder began to steal away all enjoyment at special events, which almost always involved food, as was a sign of social normalcy in America.

August 2007

I moved into my own place and began my second year of graduate work. My apartment was quaint and affordable, thanks to the assistance from my parents and aunt and my newly secured graduate assistantship in the student involvement office. I was studying communications management with a specialty in public relations and loving every moment of it. I was always a nerd like that, loving the smell of textbooks and indulging in late night study sessions until my eyes became too heavy to continue and the highlighter smell began making me woozy. I'd make thousands and thousands of notecards for study purposes, meticulously believing I would never be smart enough. I wasn't "naturally" smart like the rest of them and I could never study enough. I started making tallies for hours studied in undergrad. It wouldn't be uncommon for me to tally up to ten hours a day. I think before the eating disorder obsession, I was obsessed with studies and striving to be the best student I could possibly be. Perhaps this was a warning sign of perfectionism? I was crazy with school. Then, I became crazy with food.

When I think back to the days of living in that apartment, it literally makes me want to cry. I was so pathetic, so trapped in the life of an ED. I would obsess for hours, every morning, staring in the mirror and stepping on and off the scale. If the scale wasn't reading where I wanted it to read, I would go run for an hour and see if the number would lower. When it wouldn't, I would starve for a few days. I would take some laxatives. I would drink water and pray that the fat would disappear. I felt a high when the number on the scale was low. The lower it got, the higher I felt. But, it was NEVER enough. It was NEVER low enough. And, by the time it was low enough to be acceptable in my mind, my body was so starved that I would "binge" (later to find my binge was not nearly enough for a marathoner to ingest) and the scale would go up. After a "binge" I would then take packs (yes, packs) of laxatives until I was completely empty. The vomiting didn't start until later, when I learned that laxatives only prevented water weight gain and didn't truly rid the body of calories.

After the binge, I would literally lock myself in my apartment bedroom for days. Dark and desperate, I remember calling my parents and crying. My stomach would be in knots and my head would throb from the dehydration effects of the laxatives. My eyes would be bloodshot and I'd turn my phone to silent, blocking out the world and worrying those around me. To think of the pain and worry I caused my parents is almost too much to handle. Looking back, I can't imagine being my mom or dad during those days. Here I was, a 24-year-old young woman, starving myself to death and continually hurting my body, my soul, to no avail. Nothing was helping and though one day I'd seem fine, the next I could "binge" and lock myself away, shutting out the world and sending texts about how I wanted to die. How the world would be a better place without me.

I now understand that my depression was forming due to the eating disorder. A comorbid effect, when my brain was starved, I couldn't think logically. I remember cutting myself and taking a match to burn my hips and thighs, thinking it would burn away the fat and flesh, so I could be just bone. It hurts to write about this. In my logical and recovered mind, this makes me disgusted to think I could even think about hurting my body, the temple that God had given me.

I often have to remind myself, especially in recovery, that eating disorders are serious mental illnesses and not superficial lifestyle choices, as sometimes viewed by the media. I have to remind myself this so that the guilt of those terribly dark days and what they did to my family don't become too overwhelming.

Spring 2008

It had been about a year since I ran my first marathon, the Cleveland Rite Aid, and I was ready to run "The" Boston with my qualifying time. Mom, dad, Diane, Lee & Lynn were all there, all in one hotel room, nonetheless, to support my endeavor. I restricted the whole time. Knowing my body would need the nourishment to make the twenty-six miles without breaking down my muscle for fuel, I decided to nibble on some salad and breadsticks the evening before the race. The night before that, we went to the Boston Red Sox game. I skipped dinner and ate a few peanuts. My eating disorder had me by the throat. I was surrounded by thin runners, some of the most successful endurance athletes in the nation. The only way I could succeed, according to ED, was to starve myself and purge any excess body weight in the few days before the race.

Somehow, God was with me, and I finished the race only five minutes slower than my personal record, despite "Heartbreak Hill" and the massive amounts of people. It was thrilling. I'll never forget the crowds, the screaming college girls through Wellseley around mile 12 and the feeling of extreme accomplishment as I crossed those feet over the finish line. I did the Boston marathon two more times, in 2009 and 2010. I couldn't get enough. Then, my body began to rebel.

October 2008

I was able to wrap up my master's degree through an independent study in the fall of 2008, allowing me to take a job at my alma mater and move down to Columbus, OH and move in with my sister, Lynn, to a quaint townhouse and her beautiful golden retriever. I was sad to leave all my wonderful friends at home, but I was excited for the chance and opportunity to start this next chapter of my life, hopefully ED free.

Instead, unfortunately, with the changes in lifestyle, surroundings, and work, I turned to ED, just as bad as ever. Lynn was naturally thin. Part of my ED was comparing myself to others. I became obsessive in comparing myself with Lynn. When she ran 3 miles, I had to run 7. When she ate a lean cuisine for lunch, I ate a jelly bean. That was part of my obsession. Comparing myself to others and feeling inadequate. Because of these feelings of inadequacy, I turned to food and exercise to try and be better than others, in the one thing I felt I could. It was so backwards and messed up, but that's what my mind kept telling me. I'll never be good enough. I'll never be thin enough. I'll never be smart enough. I'll never excel. BUT, I can starve myself. And, I can run another mile. Somehow, it made me feel better. Then, I would binge. It was a vicious cycle.

When I binged, I would take packs of laxatives and lay in bed in severe pain. I would miss work. I would miss life. I couldn't bear to be seen when my stomach was full of food. It was my sign of failure and weakness; I would hide under the covers until my body was entirely purged of any and all calories. These days were dark. I'd call and text my family and tell them I was having a "bad day". They learned to know what this meant. I'd be entirely negative and hopeless, saying things like I wish I was dead. I was a fat, useless being who only caused worry and anger. It didn't matter what day it was, whether it was mother's day or Easter, my sister's birthday or my friend's bachelorette party.

If it was a bad day, it was a bad day, and I was NOT going to leave my bed. No one deserved to see me in this state, I thought. My stomach protruding, my eyes bloodshot, my thighs expanding and my behind bulging: I was in the depth of my ED, and I wasn't leaving.

November 2009

I started dating John. We went to the movies and out for a drink, and I finally had an 'aha' moment, where I knew we should be together. After months of thinking about it, I finally decided I wanted to date him. I thank him for putting up with my stubbornness. You see, I think I was scared to try it, because I didn't want to mess it up. He was a great friend. Little did I know that one day, he would be a main motivator in recovery.

June 2009

I got t-boned by a woman texting on her phone today. She made a left turn into me on a green light, didn't even slow down. Speeding into my driver's side front door at 55 miles per hour, I remember looking up to God (as time seemed to freeze) and thinking, 'this is it...I'm going to die. Please Lord, I am sorry and please let my family know how much I love them'. Somehow, I survived.

To this day, I think it took this moment, of my life literally flashing before my eyes, to realize I needed help. Life was so fragile and unpredictable; I didn't want to live another day of it with an ED. Funny how small tragedies can be blessings in disguise, huh? Thankfully, I was driving a large jeep, which, according to the doctor's is probably the only reason I made it out alive. My car was destroyed, entirely totaled. The airbag crushed my knees and my arm was gushing blood, but my body kept strong, and I made it through with only slight injuries. I, to this day, often pray for that woman, who was driving uninsured with two children in her backseat while texting. They were all unharmed, minus precautionary trips to the hospital for symptoms of whiplash. God is good. I needed to prove that he saved my life for a reason. He gave me a second chance. The second chance needed ED gone.

October 2010
I was stubborn until the very end of pre-treatment life. After the car accident, I called Remuda Ranch treatment center several times, due to a recommendation from a dear friend and running companion, but could not afford their package. The numbers were too high and it wasn't possible. I continued to train for a marathon and actually ran one a week prior to leaving for Remuda (you'll see below that somehow, someway, I was able to get a

generous grant to go to Remuda). At mile 25 my body failed me. I almost think it was to humor me. I had made it this far, but without getting help, I wasn't going to make it to the end. I had to walk for about 10 minutes and sit down to regain composure and vision. I finished the race, but I knew it was time for professional help, come hell or high water.

Inpatient Treatment

On October 2, 2010 I went to a healing service with my mom. It was held up in the Cleveland area by Dr. N, who had been practicing medicine for over 20 years, but that was beside the point. He was a Saint; he was truly able to connect with the Lord and bring the Holy Spirit to each person he touched. I, being mad at God and putting my faith on the back burner with the eating disorder taking over every aspect possible, didn't really believe it. I told my mom that I would go – she had been suggesting it for months – but a few hours before the service, I began to cry and surrender, pleading not to go. We went. I'm glad.

Though a miracle didn't occur the evening of the service and I still went against any hope that tried to seep through my mind, I did notice an immediate and innate physical change. Being cursed with scoliosis since puberty, my spine had always been crooked and my hips had always been uneven. My oldest sister, Diane, had it worse than me, and had to get corrective surgery her sophomore year of high school, complete with a steel rod. I luckily stopped growing in the niche of time and my curvature fell just below the border that called for surgical intervention. When it was my mom and I's turn, we walked slowly up to the front line, waiting for Dr. N to put his hands on our forehead. We waited for him to say a prayer over us and bless us with the Holy Spirit. Some people had collapsed and swore they were taken completely out of reality, grasped in the Holy Spirit for those few moments. My mom was one of them. She said she felt heat and warmth overtake her body and she collapsed. I didn't. I was resilient and still somewhat of a non-believer. I was stubborn and bitter with God. Dr. N, though, didn't give up on me. He spent a good amount of time praying, talking, praying some more. He said I would be about an inch taller, that my spine was corrected. Indeed, it was. I was sore; my spine had moved; and being 5' 8 ¼" was history. Now, I was 5' 9".

Two weeks later, I was granted an opportunity to go get help at a well-known inpatient facility, known as Remuda Ranch, in Wickenburg, Arizona. Since its inception in 1990, Remuda has treated 10,000 individuals with eating disorders, boasting a high recovery rate. The CEO granted me a huge amount of money to make my treatment possible. He looked at my case and made it happen. Trekking across the country completely alone was a scary feat, but I knew I had to do it. I was willing to take that chance. I would be staying there for 45 days, having no idea what I was about to experience. The depth of the eating disorder was rooted in my soul, and it was time to yank it out. Following, you'll see my daily musings, for 45 days, with corresponding entries from my mother's point of view. While I was in Arizona, she was in Cleveland, Ohio, but each night we saw the same moon. We were still connected, even on opposite sides of the country, and that made all the difference.

Meggie's Journal (daily musings while at inpatient treatment)

October 23, 2010, Day #3

Okay, so I fibbed a little. Great credibility for my authorship, right? Well, I didn't write all 45 days. The first days were just too overwhelming. This entry really counts for three days, though. I spent hours writing in my journal, desperate and isolating, wanting to escape in the worst way and quietly crying to myself. The first few days were nothing short of misery.

I've been at Remuda two days now and can single-handedly say it's been the toughest two days of my life. From monitored meals to being stripped of all adult privileges, exercise and control, I feel trapped and helpless. The boredom is sinking in as I'm so entirely programmed to the "on-the-go" lifestyle, full of stress and crunch time, long runs and people-pleasing. I can't wait to be back! My stomach is slowly adjusting. The amount of food and spaced timing is something I haven't done in five years. It's so foreign to me. I feel controlled, like a little puppeteer. The rules, to me, are silly. They have to flush my toilet after mealtime to make sure I haven't purged. They took away my make-up because it had a mirror. They took away half my running shirts because the influence of exercise could be triggering to some. They even took away a t-shirt that said "Cherry Coke". No internet, no cell phone, and no phone (period) for the first 72 hours. I came into this fast and somewhat blindly. I can say it's been harder, more emotional and worse than I had ever expected or thought it could possibly be. I feel like my mental and physical health will turn to mush. Hardly any mental stimulation and absolutely no exercise allowed? It seems unreal, unfair and completely unrealistic. My muscles will deteriorate and I'm so scared...BUT...

Let's look at the positives. I need to be strong, proud and happy that I made this huge step toward recovery. A recovery, I realized, I just couldn't do without professional and controlled help. My environment at home was supportive, especially with my sister Lynn (who I lived with) and John (my boyfriend of a year, at the time I entered treatment), but I could still get away with uncontrolled, eating disordered style of day to day life. I could restrict, skip and eventually binge and purge. "Good" days (days when I starved or ate a rice cake or two) were counteracted by "bad" days (days where I ate a whole box of cereal). Happiness was drowned with sadness, due to guilt associated with the disorder. I was never free of sad thoughts, regardless if I was with the love of my life or on a beach vacation with my loving family. I've promised myself, this will all CHANGE.

I need to regain stability and happiness. This won't truly happen until I'm rid of the disorder. Though I may not ever be 100% freed, I know I will be on the right track after this. Though I'm sacrificing fun, a social life, two of my great friend's weddings, time with my best friend and love of my life (John), and Halloween and Thanksgiving, it will be worth it if it promises for a healthier, happier future with marriage and kids, stability and success professionally. I know it seems like the end of the world right now, and basically it is, but I need to take it a day at a time, embrace it and take deep breaths.

While I'm at this, perhaps I can even write a book one day, a book that can assist other young women struggling with such an all-encompassing disease. I don't know what's in store for the next 43 days, but I do know that I will survive. It is going to be tough and heart-breaking, intense yet extremely boring, but I just have to look at it as a time of rest and recovery from the damage I've managed to do to myself. Though I feel least in need of all these ladies here, I know there's a reason God has me here. There's a reason I was given this opportunity, with all the stars aligning and pointing me here. I guess I'm scared most right now to let go and have a change occur. I don't want to come back a different person; although, I know the core of me that has blossomed in the past 26 years will be unshaken; the only change that will occur will be ridding my body of this awful disease, one that has engrained itself in every grain of my being for the past five years. As John says, it has its claws in me and it's time to obliterate them...forever. Another thing I'm dealing with – many of the girls are younger here, some still 18 years, including my roommate. Most are no older than 23 years. It's hard to relate as I have a completely different aspect on life. One woman though, Kim, has become my mentor and guardian angel these first few days. She leaves in eight days, but such is the nature of this place. I told her how jealous I was of her short time left. She laughed and said she earned it. She has been in the 60 day program. We talked about how out of shape we will both be upon our return, as we're both somewhat obsessive runners/exercisers, but we just have to accept it; there's literally nothing else we can do. Best of all, Kim lives in Columbus! She has suffered with an eating disorder for many years. She makes sure I'm okay and oftentimes distracts me with games of Bananagrams. She is a quiet soul, sweet-natured and serene. She's beautiful, too. If she could do this and come out on top, I will make that my end goal, too.

I was also able to meet my therapist yesterday. He (yes, HE!) is going to be an angel, too. Down-to-earth, real and a male, he will be just what I need to vent and collect my thoughts in a one-on-one basis. It's hardest to feel trapped with no control, and he *totally gets that.* He'll bring a sense of the real world with him, as we've already started conversations about the Ohio State Buckeyes and how bad they screwed up last week!

I just talked to Kim more. I love how she has opened up to me. She says my body will change, but that it's best to just embrace it. Clothes might fit differently, but that's okay. I will be back to my natural self, the one pre-disorder. With the disorder, I've lost, gained, lost, gained, and stayed stable, noticed bloating and restoration of fat during stages of bulimic behaviors. Once I get on a stable, normal schedule, my body will readjust, jump start my metabolism and relearn how to burn calories appropriately. I can only imagine the freedom of being in my own skin and accepting my natural shape. Going out to lunch at work and out to dinner with John? Unheard of! No feelings of guilt or shame or obsession to go run or restrict to balance it all out. I can only hope and pray that one day, one day *soon*, I will be able to do this wholly, completely and honestly.

No longer will I restrict until so ravaging hungry that I feel urges to binge and then repercussions to purge. I can do this and *will* do this. It's snack time now, but I haven't yet met with my dietician to determine how many points (EQ/equivalents) I will need to do. So, today, I don't think I'll take it. Not yet. Little by little.

This afternoon we did some art therapy, some skills class and recreational therapy, which included "noodle hockey" and a "rock" game of sorts. Like I said, I feel like I'm treated like a baby and my mental and physical capacities are being stripped from me, but emotional focus is right now and that's the way it needs to be. I need to take these days to equip myself with the strength and skills to make it in the future –career-wise, socially, physically, with John, for my family- and for the good of everything and everyone, not just myself. It's only one and one half months of my entire life. I'm already thinking about how I will view my life upon my return – how blessed I will feel to have my freedom, my adult privileges, my loved ones all within my reach. I will see the value and cherish more what all I have.

Relearning what a normal meal is and what a normal caloric intake is throughout the day is incredibly tough, guilt-stricken but eye-opening all the same. If I keep having free time with little to do,

I honestly think I'll be able to produce a novel by the end of this (my intuition served me right).

I'm hoping my Family Week will be the fourth week, which I think would be November 14th or 21st (more about family week to come, but basically it's getting to the root of my eating disorder with the support and feedback from the ones I love most, my parents). It's sad but what I most look forward to these past couple of days is sleep at night. Just sleep, silence, no thinking, no worrying, obsessing or dealing with loud and immature 18-year-olds (some of which became like sisters down the road- funny how things change!). One side of me is thankful that I never had to deal with such a disease at such a young age; another side of me is upset that it has to interrupt my life at this point. It's frustrating that everything had to be put on hold, but I must trust and believe that I'm meant to be here, to learn, to progress to a fuller (both literally and figuratively), happier and accepting self.

I'm terrified about how my body might change and fearful of gaining even more weight. My dietician said she can tell my body fat is too low and she may have to supplement me in addition to the "maintenance" diet. Apparently the food they provide us is meant only to maintain our weight, not make us gain. So to get "weight restoration" (as they so sneakily call it), they provide "supplements," which means either a feeding tube at night or ensure supplement shakes throughout the day. I CANNOT AND WILL NOT believe that I need to gain weight. She said 125 is not healthy, though, in my mind that's my highest acceptable weight at 5' 9". She said 135 (the heaviest I had ever been) wasn't even healthy. I'm unsure what this means and hope and pray she just guides me to the right direction and pulls me through all this doubt. I will say that eating throughout the day has completely erased the urge for any type of binge. No interest in that, which, I know is a good thing.

Thinking of going off the "gentle" diet freaks me out. They are "nice" the first couple of days and don't make you eat as much. Eating solid, heavy foods makes me feel like I'll blow up. I'm so used to eating only one meal and all at once and then skipping days. Again, I know this schedule leads to trouble and bad days. This is the best way for me to break it. I can, and I will. I just feel my mood is kind of down, up, back down right now, which I suppose is really due to adjusting and feeling completely controlled and out of my comfort zone. My goal right now is just to make it to week 3. Then I have family week right ahead and it winds down from there. Then, I GET MY LIFE BACK, and Christmas is right around the corner, my favorite time of the year.

Another new admittance came this evening. She's another 18-year-old. Kim and I don't quite understand because there is an adolescent ranch that seems more sufficient. So, I hear tomorrow is another "down" day, so I'll probably be writing in quite a bit once again. Hoping once the week starts, I'll be more active and busy. I know exercise won't be a reality – which simply SUCKS- but I have to keep strong.

Day #4, October 24, 2010

Today has been up and down again, but I was able to talk to mom, John and my middle sister, Lynn, which was obviously the highlight of my stay here so far. They are three of my strongest rocks and biggest supporters. So, this journal here, it is going to be turned into a book, perhaps not one for publishing, but one for mom and me. She promises to write a journal from her perspective as I write mine. I will eventually compile it as somewhat of a mother/daughter journey through recovery. When I talked to John, I loved talking about the plan and reminding myself that the metabolism will counteract the change in food structure and habit. He talks honestly and openly (and always has) and reminds me it will be okay. We talked about how hard it's going to be not to have each other to hold the next weeks, but I know in my heart our relationship will be stronger than ever once I get back. No more bad days due to the disorder. Yes, other relationship problems will likely pop up, but this will be one less thing, and it was the main factor in the majority of our arguments. I'm so blessed to have a sister like Lynn, one to look after home and my kitty, Gracie, and everything else while I am away. We agreed the six weeks will fly by and we talked about the dinners we will have when I return; how we will be able to enjoy meals together and even go out to eat once and awhile. It's eye-opening to even think this will be possible. Chapel is at 2 p.m. today, which I am happy about. I need God for this journey.

I found some quotes posted around the ranch. I like the little tidbits of hope strategically sprinkled around the room:

"What we think, we become."

"And the day will come when the pain of staying the same will outweigh the fear of changing." (One of my all-time favorite quotes, being so applicable to eating disorder recovery).

"Nothing great has been and nothing great can be accomplished without passion."

"If you see someone without a smile, give them yours."

"True beauty is being yourself."

Day #5, October 25, 2010

Today, I'm okay. It's Monday, so I'm hoping they will be able to move me to at least yellow, if not green status, so I'm able to fully participate in all activities. It's such an elementary idea; a simple use of negative reinforcement, but it works. They put us on a wristband system (red to yellow to green) depending on medical stability and dietary compliance. I'm tired of being bored and tired of just being stuck inside the ranch. I must say that physically, I'm feeling better. Eating throughout the day is going to stabilize my mood. The trick is letting go of the guilt and shame associated with the act of nourishment, something normal and pure for the human body. I have to accept any and all changes of my body associated with this nourishment. My natural body structure, shape and composition are beautiful. I must believe this. My one major concern is no exercising, but after the years of constant running, I'm sure realistically my body could use the rest, regardless. I just have to remind myself how strong and healthy I will be once I return to the races.

Cee Cee is another sweetheart I've met. She is 23 and from Colorado. She has been struggling since high school and is on the same page as me. She initiated her stay here and wants recovery. She wants that normal, healthy lifestyle complete with a family. She is so determined; in fact, she has single-handedly decided to do weight restoration options in addition to the maintenance diet. She allowed feeding tube intervention in the evenings. She explained that to completely and utterly let go of ED, she would need to listen to the dietician's suggestion. Indeed, she has struggled with this, but she is such a strong and beautiful young woman. We agreed we will keep each other positive throughout our stay.

Turns out my dietician wants me to take supplements or feeding tube intervention, too, for this thing they like to call "weight restoration". Seems foreign, unrealistic and silly to me, but apparently my body fat and muscle mass are too low. This freaks me out and provides lots of anxiety. I am already anxious and fearful of three meals a day plus three snacks, but added ensures throughout the day just makes me want to hurl. Compared to Cee Cee, I should NOT have to do this. Today's lessons focused much on the roots of my problem, which are masked by the behaviors of my eating disorder. We met as a group today – Home Group C – to hear Cee Cee's "life story" (a project each of us endures to see if themes and revelations appear related to our eating disorders). Her bravery continues to inspire me.

Day #6, October 26, 2010

"If we don't make internal change, the disease either comes back or we create another disease."

A few breaths of fresh air I'd like to share that happened over the past couple of days. First, Chapel last night was soothing, comforting and inspiring. I felt wholly and fully there because I wasn't starving or worrying about what I had eaten. Having no control is horrid, yet comforting all in the same. I don't have a choice, so I must embrace and eat what is provided. I am also being told I must restore some pounds with supplements, a major source of anxiety for me, and yet I am not ready to surrender to this yet. Only time will tell.

This morning, having been moved to yellow status, I was able to partake in morning stretch. Being the exerciser that I am, I will certainly do that, and I'm hoping I can start cardio walk and form (a very gentle form of yoga) on Sundays. Cardio walk will be M-W-F 6 a .m. to 6:30 a.m. and stretch will be T-R 6:30 am to 6:50 a.m. (This wish was never granted). It was nice to stretch the muscles that are quickly atrophying. It might just be in my head, but I feel they are. The nurse just shouted that Prince William will be announcing his engagement. Anyways, it's a bit like a bubble here. No outside world blitz and chaos, which I miss and don't miss at the same time.

Also, the strangest thing, I've been eating full and solid meals and embracing and adjusting. I started the day with oatmeal, a whole wheat blueberry muffin and peaches; something I never would have dreamed of doing just one week ago. I believe lunch is tomato soup and a turkey sandwich. I can't say that I feel confident and comfortable, but I can say I hope it gets easier as each day passes. Last night, I was able to talk to dad, mom, and Mister John. Dad always seems to make me cry, but in a good way. He explained his feeling of pride that I finally came to terms with this and his letter, of course, said "You're a FERAN! You are strong." Mom talked about how the moon outside was the same moon in both Arizona and Ohio. It is watching over both of us, regardless of difference in location. She wrote that her heart swells with the amount of love she has for me. John said he hasn't been feeling great – migraines – and I'm praying it's not due to worry about his mom or even me maybe. He talked about how he waited around the phone since 8:30 p.m. and looked forward to my call. That made me feel good. He talked about how he'll be tutoring two college students in economics the next two nights to keep busy. He's such a good guy. He already mentioned how he will be stocking his place with all the food to follow my diet plan so it's at my fingertips. We can eat together and he can eat similarly for support. I'm going to marry this man one day.

Day #7, October 27, 2010

I've almost survived a whole week, imagine that! Today was my first day of supplement – a thick, chocolate ensure. Yuck. I'm a little down right now having just drank that and being controlled to have lunch in less than one hour. I can feel the calories and no exercise making me even less energetic, but, alas, I will let my body take this time for nourishment for what it is worth, trusting in God and this opportunity. I just met with Dr. M, a psychologist, to review some assessments and my background. It felt good to vent about perfectionism and living/growing up with extremely health-conscious and exercise-heavy mom and Diane. I'd never blame anyone but me, but I do admit these tendencies have become engrained in my mind. It was my own fault to push it to the extreme, though. This morning we had group therapy, which focuses on "feeling checks" and "checking in" on others. I also was able to do stretch and had cereal, toast and an orange for breakfast. I'm still scared and obsessed over how my body will change due to all this solid food, but I recognize my body feeling healthy and full in a way it hasn't in quite some time.

Every night after snack, it's time for devotional. Julie has been in charge this week and last night her scripture reading really struck me. She talked about how God created and crafted us in the womb and we were made good enough and perfectly in our own way, in God's creative image. I just ate snack now, though, and I'm feeling down, overwhelmed, stressed and sad. I'm bloated and emotional. I had a conversation about not being able to run and it has me down and out. I looked at my reflection during equine and comparatively speaking, I'm obese and large. The girls are young and loud and my friend Kim leaves in just two days. I'm scared about the future days and more changes. I have a nutrition class and chapel after this, so I'm hoping it gets my mind off things and in a more hopeful mood. I have lunch with the dietician tomorrow, and I will talk to her about the supplements and how uncomfortable I feel about this. Two and ½ weeks until mom will be here, my saving grace and hope. Just to hold and see her, be by her side and remember and feel the love and hope – that's what I want. Dad, my hero and my inspiration – I can't wait to hug him. And, possibly John can come during "pass" weekend (the ranch's idea of freedom without food chains) so I can see him for a bit, get away, hold him and know he's going to be there for me when I get back. It's the reassurance, acceptance, and love that keep me going. Too bad I have such a long way to go.

Day #8, October 28, 2010

A new day; a new dawn; a new beginning. I started the day as usual with vitals, menu selection, electric shaving (we are not allowed to have real razors for fear of self-harm) and hair straightening. We're kind of treated like we're in a jail, to be perfectly honest. I haven't had a bowel movement in two days (I know, GROSS!) and have been eating A LOT! I think my system is still in shock and still holding onto all the fat and nutrients that it hasn't been blessed with in quite some time. At 8:15 a.m. we have body image class. John sometimes says that I have a distorted image and I do believe that this may be true, but saying or thinking that I'm thin or average is still far, far, far from reality.

Two of the stick figure thin girls (whom I so jealously envy) are at the menu selection screen again; obsessing over the three options we are given. They always do that together; they must think they might be able to cheat the system and choose the no calorie, no fat, and no nutrient selections. I wish. I've already somewhat surrendered to the fact that I'm going to have to eat here. There's nothing I can do about. It's just for 45 days. By no means will I plan to continue on this large amount of calories with no exercise (which, I really needed to do…), but I will plan to healthily tailor my life to be more balanced and less obsessive. I must do this for sanity and peace. Some girls here don't want to let go of ED. I feel stress and insecurity because of it. It makes me feel like I do NOT need to be here in the first place when I stand next to all the skinny girls. Rather, I should be in FAT camp. I don't need to add weight, certainly (CERTAINLY!) not. I know this isn't the right mentality and I understand it may mean I have plenty of work left to do, but I will continue to pray, to see the light, and to keep my eye on the prize – health, happiness, marriage and children with John. Yes, I can do this, and I will do this. I'm determined and will do my best to make today a good day. I must say at times I feel this was such a drastic decision and unnecessary, but then I think of how I felt – the guilt, restrictions, secret night binges and purges, obsessive runs – and I pull myself back together, centered and reminded that this was necessary, completely and utterly necessary. I think of my constant focus on food – which still hasn't disappeared- and I know gosh life is SO much more than this, SO much more.

Body image class was good. We learned about cultural influence on body ideals. It's amazing to see how much social influence can affect disordered eating. Bombarded with subliminal messaging of thinness, exercise, perfection, strength, it's no wonder our youth- being the susceptible sponges that they are- soon incorporate sickened habits and tendencies in day to day life. It's disheartening but reversible. I want to get on the bandwagon one day, when returned to health, to curtail this downward spiral leading to anorexia and bulimia. Tonight, I'll call my sister Lynn. I haven't talked to her since Sunday and I need her to send some normalcy vibes and practical items: lip gloss, powder sans mirror (self-harm, again), warm socks/booties, pictures and a Bible.

I just met with the medical doctor, and she said I'll have a follow-up EKG tomorrow. Upon arrival I have something called a prolonged PCB, which is an effect of purging behaviors. They drew some blood and will check on electrolyte imbalance. I had lunch with the dietician, and she suggested I work on writing a letter to my running shoes or to the trails and why I need a break from them – a break like from an unhealthy relationship, one that has contributed to my eating disordered behavior. I will attempt to do this but can almost guarantee that after five more weeks of no running, I'll be more than ready and anxious to hit the trails. I know I need to do it healthily, but I know it's part of who I am, part of my identity and being. I don't have a desire to give that up, either. Chapel was pretty tonight and the speaker gave us a song to try and repeat to ourselves three times per day when we were feeling down (how about 3,333,333 times per day?), as that's how many times I feel down in the dumps, lately.

Beautiful
Days will come when you don't have the strength
When all you hear is you're not worth anything
Wondering if you ever could be loved
And if they truly saw your heart, they'd see too much.

You're beautiful. You're beautiful.
You are treasured. You are sacred.
You are His. You're beautiful.
Praying that you have the heart to fight
Because you're more than what is hurting
For all the lies you've hid inside so long
They are nothing in the shadow of the cross.

You're beautiful. You're beautiful.
You are made for so much more than all of this.
You're beautiful. You're beautiful.
You are treasured. You are sacred.

You are His. You're beautiful.
Before you ever took a breath,
Long before the world began.
Of all the wonders He possessed there was one
more precious.
Of all the earth and skies above
You're the one He madly loves
Enough to die.

You're beautiful. You're beautiful.
In his Eyes.

Day #9, October 29, 2010

Today I awoke to FRIDAY. Normally, I'd be content and excited for this day to finally arrive, but today I'm not. I know it foreshadows the dullness and monotony of the weekend, lacking programming and providing down-time and lots and lots of reflection. I received a nice letter from Diane and my brother-in-law yesterday and a package from Lynn with Cover Girl powder! Yay! No more greasy "concealer-only" face. My brother-in-law reminded me of the control that lie within me and how the support of therapists, dieticians, etc. only get me so far before I need to reach to the power within. The power to fully recover for myself, my future, and my happiness all lies directly within me.

I'll have a repeat EKG done today and I'm constantly reminded of my low heart rate – it ranges usually between 41 and 45 beats per minute. They originally thought this was a bad sign but now realize I'm a runner and a low heart rate is typical. I will also meet with our community group and go to chapel tonight (my favorite part of the day). I need to write my "life story" this weekend, a project we all do to process with our families. Family Week is quickly approaching. It will happen either November 7th or November 14th. I'm somewhat rooting for the 14th so I have a bit more time to grow and reach for thoughts and beliefs that have led to my actions of disordered eating. Mom said I should be receiving a package today with books. This will be a nice distracter, too.

Eating, eating, eating and uncomfortable with my body. I could write each item every day, though I know mentally this isn't a wise decision, so I will not. Obsessing and bloating and scared of the next five weeks, but hopeful and just realized there's a computer where I can perhaps type the writings so far and chip away at this book. Honestly, I don't know if I'll have the time or passion to relive this experience once I return to Columbus (I did). I read a passage in the book Captivating: Unveiling the Mystery of a Woman's Soul, by John and Stasi Eldredge that struck me today and reminded me of the importance and legitimacy of times of suffering:

"To possess true beauty, we must be willing to suffer. "

I don't like that sentence. Just writing it down makes my heart shrink. Yet, if Christ himself was perfected through his sufferings, why would I believe God would not do the same to me? Women who are stunningly beautiful are women who have had their hearts enlarged by suffering. "By saying "yes" when the world says "no"; by paying the high price of loving truly and honestly without demanding that they be loved in return; and, by refusing to numb their pain in the myriad of ways available. They have come to know that when everyone and everything has left them, God is there. They have learned, along with David, that those who go through the desolate valley will find it a place of springs." (p. 143)

This week, I've learned help skills, including accepting, willingness, wisdom, distracting, feeling, acting opposite, catching it, and caring. Acceptance is acknowledging the reality of what is, what has been, making the conscious decision to accept that certain things are the way they are; certain things have happened the way they happened. This is life. Willingness means focusing on what is needed in the moment, one step at a time, moment-by-moment. A statement that helps me be willing, for the most part in relation to supplements and no exercise, is "the most that I have to lose by fully cooperating with my treatment team's recommendations for me while I'm here is 45 to 60 days of my entire life. Virtually everything that I do while in treatment can be undone if I desire to undo it at the end of my treatment journey. I can try things out, experiment, give them a trial run – for 45 to 60 days."

Today's chapel message was: "Be Still." This place is making me, (okay, quite frankly, forcing me), to learn that mantra. In fact, it's quite brilliant.

Day #10, October 30, 2010

I had some strange dreams last night. I haven't had dreams I could remember for quite some time. Perhaps it's because I've been nutritionally sound for the last week. When I look in the mirror, I appear about the same, which I'm ashamed of. Not confident or comfortable in my own skin. Maybe one day this will change but right now, that's unforeseeable. I refuse to take two additional supplements, which is upwards of 550-600 calories additional to what I'm assuming is 1800 daily caloric intake via food already. It still seems unreal and unfair to my body to endure such a drastic change.

This morning I had a great conversation with Cee Cee. We are very similar in our thinking and it's so nice to have someone with whom to relate. We will be having family week together since mine has been bumped up to November 7th. John will be here November 11th through the 14th, giving me hope and peace of mind.

We went to the nature preserve and walked around for a bit, and then did art therapy where I made a heart box for my mom with a serenity cross and bright yellow center. She's been my ray of sunshine from the beginning of all this. Speaking of which, let's transition to the first few days from my mother's perspective, through her voice, as written in her journal and shared with me upon the birthday following my release from treatment.

My Mother ... {her journal while I was away at Remuda}.

"This journal belongs to Mom. A gift to me from Meggie. I am keeping this journal while Meggie is at Remuda Ranch and in recovery..."

The journal theme held my mom's favorite scripture and poem, which certainly related to the content about which it was about to hold and about which I am about to share to you. In case you're unfamiliar with this poem, it goes like this:
One night I dreamed I was walking along the Beach with the Lord.
Many scenes from my life flashed across the sky.
In each scene I noticed footprints in the sand.
Sometimes there was one set of footprints.
It bothered me because I noticed that during the Low periods of my life,
When I was suffering from anguish, sorrow and Defeat, I could see only one set of footprints.
So, I said to the Lord, "You promised me, Lord, that If I followed You, you would walk with me always,
But I noticed that during the most trying periods of My life, there have only been one set of footprints In the sand.
Why, when I have needed you the most, You have Not been there for me?"
The Lord replied,

"The times when you have seen only one set of footprints, is when I carried you."

10/21/2010, Day #1

Today is a new beginning for Meggie, our family, and John. Meggie is on a flight to Remuda Ranch in Phoenix where she will begin a 45-day treatment for her eating disorder. Meggie has struggled with the disorder for five years. It has been hard on her both mentally and physically. It has affected our family as well. We are a very close family filled with love for each other, so to see Meggie struggle with this has been difficult for all of us.

I believe Meggie's prayers for healing were answered when we went to a healing service with Dr. N on October 2. I believe she received a miracle. Meggie looked into Remuda Ranch earlier in the summer. At that time, it was not affordable to our family. Somehow (and here's the miracle), funds became available from Remuda and we were able to afford the rest. I will end my entry today with a quote from Path to Faith (Dr. N's blog): "Jesus is the Healer and His Holy Spirit affects the healing because The Father wants it at this moment in your life." God has a plan. There is a reason Meggie has had this struggle. She has had amazing accomplishments with this disorder – I can only imagine what she will do when she is healed.

10/24/2010

I have so many thoughts going through my head. I am going to randomly write them down as I remember them –

- Meggie sat on the plane from Columbus to Atlanta (before connecting to Arizona) with Jack Hanna and his wife, from the Columbus Zoo.

- I talked to M (from now on, M equals Meggie) on her layover in Atlanta. She sounded good, which made me feel better. The treatment center has been M's idea. She knows this is what she needs, no matter how difficult. So, she has accepted it, and her strength and determination is in her voice.

- I talked to John. John is M's soul mate. He wants her better and supports her 100%. I love John. M told me it would mean a lot to have John at Family Week (more about Family Week later). I talked to John about it. He wants to be there for her. Financially, he would not be able to do it. We will get John there. I think knowing M will get to see John will keep her spirits up.

- I spoke to M's nurse, Jan, Friday afternoon. She said they started M on vitamins and calcium. The primary care doctor was examining M now. She said M came to breakfast as soon as she was called. She said it's overwhelming when they first arrive, but M seemed to be doing fine. I told her she would love M.

- I got a phone call from M's therapist Friday evening. We will be setting up a phone appointment of 30-45 minutes to give him our perspective, and so he can explain the treatment he has in mind. I am very impressed with Remuda Ranch. It is top-notch and very professional.

- I feel more a part of the healing process. They are keeping us informed and helping us to help M.

- When M and I went to see Dr. N, I wondered what miracle I might receive. Maybe I'd receive better hearing? I figured it out. My miracle is M's miracle, one in the same. I e-mailed Kathy, his wife, about M's miracle. I asked her and Dr. N to continue praying for

M. I received an e-mail back saying they will continue to pray for her complete recovery.

10/25/2010

I had a pleasant surprise. M called me early today right as I was getting ready to leave for church. She broke down at first, but I think it was just being able to talk to us again. For the first 72 hours, no communication with family or friends is allowed. John said she also burst into tears upon hearing his voice. John's voice is one of his best qualities, along with his smile.

After the initial breakdown, she sounded wonderful. She brought me up to speed about her first 72 hours. It actually had not been exactly 72 hours yet, but she sweet talked the nurse into letting her use the phone a little bit sooner. Weekends allow for a lot of free time, which is sort of driving "Type A" M a little crazy. She feels like Monday through Friday with a regular routine will go a lot faster. They have started M off on a "gentle" diet with cream of wheat, soup, etc. She will start on a regular diet tomorrow. She says her stomach feels bloated but that is normal. I asked about her overall health. She said there might be some issues, but they can all be reversed. The hardest part for her is not being able to run or do any form of exercise. For 45 days though, she says she can tough it out.

They did say once she gets the proper nutrition she will actually become a faster runner. They said it was a miracle she was able to run marathons. Thank you, God for keeping her safe. M running marathons had become a huge concern, especially for her sister, Diane, and me. We knew her heart could stop at any moment. M's running has always been an important part for her, but Lynn, her other sister, said it became a way to cut calories, and M wasn't enjoying it anymore. I hope M stops doing marathons and returns to the running that sets her spirit and mind soaring.

Later in the evening, when I spoke to M again, she told me about the health issues. Her heart had a very slow pulse rate (41), arrhythmia and a low blood pressure. Just in the short time she has been there, though, taking in the nutrition, the tests have improved. She told me she had cream of wheat for breakfast, a turkey sandwich for lunch and macaroni and cheese and green beans for dinner. She said having the meals surrounded by the other girls was a huge support. She said she *savored* every bite, even when it made her feel full. Hearing that, made my heart sing.

She is on a 1500 calorie/day diet. She has some choices as long as she takes in that minimum among. She does not like red meat or eggs, so she can substitute ensure whenever that is being served.

10/28/10

I spoke with Dr. R on Monday, Meggie's therapist. He sounds young (M says he's in his 30s) and cute. M says he is "awesome". He was very easy to talk to. He asked me questions about our meals as a family and whether we talked about dieting. I said when the girls were younger, we sat down and ate together. Once they hit middle school and high school, they were in so many activities that things fell apart and everyone ate at different times. Dieting was not ever talked about. No one in our family needed to diet. Our only concern was if they were too skinny. Some things I shared with him about M included:

- She struggled with depression in her junior year of high school. Running and the pressure put on her by the coaches contributed to that.

- She did an independent study during her senior year at Ohio Wesleyan University (OWU) centering on the Freshman 15 phenomenon and gaining weight. She became obsessed.

- She had two close friends at OWU with eating disorders.

- Senior year at OWU, she once mentioned to me that her roommate watched everything she ate. M said she didn't get it. She ate whenever and whatever she wanted, but when she came home that summer I recognized the problem right away. She said to her sisters that living with me was hard, because I watched everything I ate. Note: I gave up sweets and junk food one Lenten season and just continued to eat that way.

- That summer, she was anorexic. I talked to her about it and said I didn't want her to go through this.

- When she lived alone in an apartment in Willoughby that was probably her most difficult time. She took sleeping pills, even laxatives. She spent days in bed.

- Then, she saw Dr. D and started taking Prozac. She moved to Columbus, OH with Lynn and seemed much better.

- M refused to take the Prozac (thinking it made her gain weight) and started to have more bad days. M did get on Prozac once more but has not been on it most recently. We feel it definitely helps her. She seems more balanced and happy when she is on it. M says it causes weight gain and that she does not want to have to rely on it the rest of her life. Dr. R says this is typical of a "Type A" personality to want to do it all by themselves; it is the perfectionist in them. I also told him she compares herself to me, Diane and Lynn. She says she wishes she looked like us. I told him Diane and are tall and lanky (actually, I think I used the term "dorky"), and Lynn is smaller-framed. That was basically my input.

Dr. R talked about Family Week. He said it is a powerful experience.

I just got back from a walk. I had to clear my head. The history was hard to write. I'm looking forward to the future, when M is healed. I wish I could put a recorder in my head; I have so many thoughts. It's hard to get them all down on paper. I thought about the most important part of the conversation with Dr. R. He asked about our relationship with M. I told him, as horrible as the disorder is, it probably made us closer. We are so bonded and have so much love for one another. If it takes love to heal M, she's got it. Our family is very close and full of love. And John – I will quote his phone text message from the other night when we were waiting for her phone call. "Yea, she just called...lol. I stare at that phone non-stop from 8 p.m. until she calls...lol." Now, that's love.

I just finished <u>The Power</u>. If you have love and give love, you can have anything. Well, we have LOVE.

Meggie's Journal { musings while at inpatient treatment, continued}

Day #11, October 31, 2010

Happy Halloween! Not quite the same when you're in an inpatient eating disorder program, but I'm still representing with my bright orange pumpkin socks and glad I don't have to face the oodles of candy surrounding the house, the office and everywhere in between. This morning I felt comfortable with my two pieces of toast (with peanut butter and grape jelly) and peaches. I feel full but not overly stuffed, and I'm slowly desensitizing and adjusting to the scheduled food regimen. The supplements, ***not so much.*** I'm supposed to do three per day and I simply cannot force myself to do this, at least not yet. If it means some privileges are reprimanded and I'm embarrassed by my inability to fully let go of my control, then so let it be. Right now, I can only do so much. I'm already disgusted by my body.

I talked to Jean this morning. She's from Massillon and a straight-forward, loveable kind of woman who is older than most others here. She has a cat named Brutus! (Go Ohio State University, Buckeyes!). Lynn's golden retriever's name is Brutus, too, so I instantly liked her. We talked about the Buckeyes football team and chatted about lupus. She has systemic lupus, which drastically affects her joints and causes inflammation and discomfort. Just like John's mom, it didn't flare up until she was in her twenties. I'll pray for her and remember her for years to come. Some people, I feel, are just like that. They touch your heart without even trying.

This week, I'll be charged with making notable quotes and inspirations on the whiteboard in the lodge. They should be a gentle reminder of why we are here. It's not about the food or the anxieties of overcoming something we've feared for so long, it's about leaning on one another as we dig deep to find the thoughts, feelings, and beliefs that have grown into ineffective habits with eating. It's so much more than the food. I've always felt shallow and guilty for having an eating disorder; it seems like such a self-centered disease from the outside. It's not. This afternoon, I'll finish my life story (documenting milestones up until my current age of 27 years) to share with my group this week and prepare for mom and dad to arrive on November 7th.

I finished my life story tonight. I thought today was off to a good start until one of the other girls unknowingly triggered and offended me. I was fearful of taking the supplement during snack time, and she said I didn't look like I needed it anyway. I wasn't drastically underweight and I looked "normal." "NORMAL." Just like I knew and told myself for months and months and months, I am NOT THIN. This triggered me to skip my supplement and then get reprimanded and embarrassed. Just want I wanted, just what I needed. I feel insecure, uncomfortable and like I'm too fat to be here. I want to cry but will instead just distract myself.

Talking to John lifted my spirits. He reminded me why I am here and although the nurses probing and prying about supplementation was unnecessary and uncomfortable, ultimately the format is like boot camp and I just have to confront the issue and deal with it. In terms of the other girl triggering me by saying I'm not underweight, such is life and to have kids, to be 27 and not 18 anymore, will mean I need to be at a healthy weight. I'm still striving for that title of ungodly thinness. I'm still scared to death.

Another uplifting moment was the cleaning personnel who told me how beautiful I was. I've gotten complimented on my long eyelashes and hair. She is so sweet.

I just got back from "form," a type of stretch done to scriptures and the Beatitudes. I feel quite out of shape and a little distant right now. I'm anxious about the upcoming week and what challenges the days will bring. I'm tiring of the rules and going stir crazy, but I know when I leave, I will be healthier and better than before…on the road to recovery and supported and trusted to take this on my own. I will use the skills and stay on the track of health with incorporation of exercise and balanced (BUT LESS THAN HERE!) meals and snacks. I feel heat flashes through the day and they say it's my metabolism flaring up. I'm hanging on….

November 1, 2010, Day #12

This morning, I got to ride Buster, the horse. Horses are such a sweet and docile species. I loved it. We did a trail walk and meandered through the sand dunes. The instructor said I needed to work on my shoulder stability with more movement in the hips as the horse walks. I could see myself falling in love with this activity; it's therapeutic and soothing. My Aunt Rae would absolutely love this. She already wrote me about taking some lessons, moving back home, and joining the posse at the Lake Farm Park with her. I'm growing, trying things I never thought realistic just a few weeks ago, and staying strong. My one consistent struggle: supplements and no exercise. I will hang in there, though, keep striving and pushing for even small steps. Perfection isn't necessary and my recovery wouldn't be real if I wasn't struggling some. I'll be meeting with the dietician, in a few minutes, and I'm scared. I will, however, stand my ground and tell her why I am not doing perfectly. She's a bit of a tough love type. She ended up telling me I needed to continue doing the supplements or I wouldn't be able to do the food challenge at Tasty Freeze with her, unless I'm 100% compliant for 72 hours. She also talked about what privileges would be taken away if I do not comply in terms of green status (it's a Remuda thing...) and family week pass. It makes me hurt, confused, terrified and scared. No one can make me do anything against my will, but the sacrifices may outweigh the price of chugging two additional fat milkshakes per day and looking like a chunky monkey by the time I get out of this joint. My wise mind tells me I don't need to gain. I just need normalcy and regulation of meals. That's it.

November 2, 2010, Day #13

"Here I am Lord..."

Nancy came from the church to give me Holy Communion and reaffirm my Catholicism. She will continue to come for the three weeks following family week. A sweet, five-minute escape to do prayer affirmations. Today I prayed for my mom, dad and John's mom, Connie. I received the Lord's body. Kim told me about this opportunity and I'm very blessed and thankful that she did so. My relationship with the Lord needs to take precedence, to give me the strength and courage toward Him and my ability to let go, to serenely trust and let go. To accept being here and accept the road to recovery, including the bumps, triggers, struggles and relapses. He will hold my hand, love me unconditionally and wholly regardless of what each day brings.

Snack time still brings the most anxiety- morning and afternoon, in particular. I can't bring myself to drinking the supplements. Enough is enough. Frustration complicated with feelings of guilt for mistrusting my treatment team. I can't go back to reality as a blimp. I simply cannot do it. I'm so scared. I know life would go on, and I could probably drop the extra pounds in a few weeks post-treatment, but the fear and anxiety complementing it, it's just TOO MUCH.

November 3, 2010, Day #14

I will share my life story today in home group, preparing for family week with mom and dad beginning on Sunday. The point of this being to find themes that may be at the root of my eating disorder.

Sharing went well with themes of perfectionism, acceptance, comparing, people pleasing and not good enough, accumulating on top. I was able to make through only crying twice, once in relation to my best friend who is also inflicted with an ED, and once in relation to the car accident/trauma I went through in June. Ricky said it seems my balance is way off kilter in terms of myself versus others. While I'd do whatever I could for others and ideally put others first in every situation, I deprive myself of basic needs. My empathy is high. Donna said I need to take my "smile mask" during my stay at Remuda and really just allow myself to struggle. I don't have to hide it here, as Donna put it, no persona and no people pleasing. The raw me. *Who am I? Why am I struggling? What needs to change?*

This afternoon is equestrian and then nutrition didactic, where we learn of appropriate portion sizing.

November 4, 2010, Day #15

I reached the two week mark today and Mom and Dad come on Sunday, so things are looking up. We just had body image class and spoke about the realities of societal and media pressures that result or influence eating disordered behaviors. It's saddening, but above all else, FRUSTRATING. We are constantly comparing ourselves to images that don't even exist. The photo shop effects and airbrush modifications are not real. Next, we have home group and I'll have a spiritual one-on-one with Ron because Dr. R isn't here. I've been working on my affirmations for my mom, dad, and John, too – laying out the positives that they've provided me, that's the easiest part. I'm continually thankful when I think about my blessed situation, circumstances, and surroundings. To be at Remuda is a blessing, and one day I want to give back. Today we watched a movie with a speaker who was once a patient at Remuda and now advocates for them. Perhaps, one day, I too will be able to do this. I would love to start a foundation, become a philanthropist in the name of females suffering with eating disorders, namely athletes.

Sometimes, while referring to my journal and writing this book, I felt a bit self-indulgent. Spending hours on the computer rather than with my John or friends or family; however, I didn't write this book to glean attention or focus on myself. Rather, I wanted to express the struggle, for not only the person with the ED, but also for his or her family. The claws dig deep. The wounds are forever. If this could save one person from getting too deep, getting help before it was too late, I was going to keep writing. And, if the reader was too far into the disorder, I wanted Remuda's name to be out there. They save lives, and I'd suggest this facility to a best friend, a sister, and even a total stranger.

Group therapy sometimes gets me in a bad mindset. There's negativity and wearing down by the other women. I just want HAPPY. Lord, please set me free. I need you.

November 5, 2010, Day #16

I am in a surprisingly good mood today and had a nice breakfast conversation with a new girl, Fran. I had a delicious toasted English muffin with margarine melted in the nooks and crannies, complemented with a vanilla and peach yogurt parfait. I ENJOYED it! Can you even believe it? We had community home group this morning and three girls gave their commitment letters for discharge. It's a way to hold themselves accountable in recovery. Last night, a few of us spoke about creating a fundraiser to raise money for girls to go to eating disorder treatment centers, namely Remuda Ranch. We decided to appropriately deem a 5k walk nationwide and try to garner support from a famous celebrity with philanthropic roots. We plan to write to Oprah, Ellen DeGeneres, and Tyra.

This afternoon, I have a lunch challenge with the dietician, who makes me panicky, but I will survive. Then, I have Bible Study at 2, followed by chapel. Mom and Dad come Sunday and I look forward to learning with them, opening my eyes and coming to terms, making complete peace with this disorder. I will win and kick ED out of the driver's seat. I'll kick it in the butt, as Cee Cee says, because I am fearlessly and beautifully made.

I have a little more downtime and then either a Family Week focus group or Bible Study followed by chapel. Next week will fly by with Family Week and then I'll begin slowly winding down from there. Recovery is a process, for certain, and I'm still far from free, but step by step, I'm embracing every day. I can and will conquer the unknown. I'm wishing this headache would dissipate; it's non-stop and annoying. Today continues to be optimistic, though, and tomorrow will entail some art therapy, recreation and mark ONE DAY until mom and dad arrive. With strength and determination, the days will fly. Focus and concentration on the skills and embracing change, though, continue to be emotionally draining. For lunch, I had a turkey and Swiss cheese sandwich, a cup of cucumber dipped in ranch, and a CHOCOLATE CHIP COOKIE. My body is adjusting and feeling vibrant with energy. I just painted my nails and they seem thicker and healthier, growing faster, thanks to the prenatal vitamins pumped into my system every morning. John sent me a note yesterday – one that touched my heart. His mom sent a note, too – which meant the world to me. We will be together forever – I know and feel it wholly and even more so with our strong bond increasing in the most difficult of times. I love him.

November 6, 2010, Day #17

Today should have been a fabulous day back on the home front. A great couple is getting married and John and I would have been there, celebrating. Alas, I'm at Remuda Ranch being punished for not fulfilling all supplements, moved to yellow status and transport, unable to ride the horses or have full privileges during pass weekend. Pass weekend was the apple to my eye. It would be free time, to get away from the ranch, and hang out with mom, dad and John. This sucks.

We are watching Home Alone and will have art therapy in about an hour. I don't mind art therapy, but I continue to get highly anxious about the supplements that haunt my day at 9:30 a.m., 2:30 p.m., and 7:45 p.m. I will not be forced to gain weight just for the sake of gaining weight when I know it's not necessary. (THIS IS ED TALKING). I'm disgusted, distraught and stressed. I came here to eat a balanced meal three times per day, have my body readjust, and awake my metabolism from years of hibernation. Even if this means I'm not

100% nutritionally compliant in their eyes, it does mean I am conquering my people-pleasing tendency to take the supplements, just to make the staff happy. I'm going to listen to God on this one – day by day and taken in stride. My recovery is my recovery. I'm paying a lot (or, at least my parents are…) to be here and will take recommendations with a grain of salt and a wise mind. I am so looking forward to hugging mom and dad tomorrow. I know I'll be crying with tears of joy, just knowing they are here and walking by my side for this next week's journey. Here are some scriptures that caught my eye today:

15:5-6 Genesis
Trust God as best you can to lead you step by step. In the end you'll find that his promises are trustworthy and that true faith has definite rewards.

11:1-9 Genesis
Perhaps you've never thought about it, but is your life like a tower of Babel? As you work each day and try to make a name for yourself, do you ever give God any credit for the good things he's given you? Do you recognize his right to have a place in your life?

Psalm 118:6
The Lord is with me: I will not be afraid. What can man do to me?

I'm hoping they will finally give me The Shack to read, as it's been over 1 ½ weeks since mom sent it. Everything must be approved and the system is slower than molasses. Being here is a lesson in patience indeed. A lesson in how blessed I am back at home – with freedom, space and the ability to FLUSH MY OWN TOILET (without being watched to make sure I don't get rid of breakfast by sticking my finger down my throat).

November 7, 2010, Day #18

I'm slowly letting go more and more, readjusting my mind to just let it be. I'm struggling but real. I'm real and honest and open that I'm not perfect in conquering this eating disorder. A way of life, my whole being and existence, for six years, may not disappear completely; however, due diligence and faith will keep me on path, following the light to health, the light to my future family and marriage with John, the soul mate who stepped into my life, who I get to celebrate one year of togetherness on Wednesday, November 10th. But this November, unlike last, I am vibrantly healthy and beautiful – full of nutrition and, therefore, full of LIFE. He lifted me up when I couldn't reach anymore, he gave me faith when I couldn't believe anymore. And, at last, I'm here at Remuda, still scared out of my mind and frightened by all the demands but strong-willed and determined to keep pushing on by the best means I am able. When I go home, the road won't be over, by any means, but the thoughts and beliefs will be more rational and stable, not so neurotic and distorted. The behaviors will not follow as strongly. I am disabling the chain reaction from the root. Mom and dad come today, and I'm praying they have a safe flight and make it here safe and sound by 2 p.m. so they can come to chapel with me. There will be ,any long hugs and tears to come. I'm so thankful.

Today I continue to be forced and twisted to the limit. I'm frustrated and losing everything. Losing any and all power; they are slowly ripping me to shreds. I'm worried and anxious and tiring of the threatening, but I can continue to push little by little. I'm just sick of being forced into something that makes my skin crawl: the supplements, of course. This afternoon, I cannot and will not do this ensure (ED TALKING, AGAIN). Today, I'm broken until dinner. No more crying and no more tears...just waiting for mom and dad, praying that they arrive so I can hug and cry. I just have to keep going.

November 8, 2010, Day #19

It's so amazing to have mom and dad here. Words cannot explain it.

I'm struggling with racing thoughts because of the supplements. I broke down yesterday, yes, but I took the supplement this morning. I still don't think I can do the one this afternoon without throwing up all the excess calories. I hope I can talk to the dietician, because I'm honestly feeling anxiety like I haven't felt before. Yes, I'm embarrassed that I'm on yellow and that my pass weekend may be decreased, but it's just my breaking point.

Mom and dad walked around with me yesterday. I showed the horses and the cross, then we went down and sat by the bunkhouse (where all the girls sleep at night). We were happy, living in the moment. We are hopeful. Today we had an orientation. My dad, of course, kept the mood light by sneaking a snack into the group room and laughing as a lone peanut tumbled into the aisle. It will be a good week. The rest will fly by minus the supplements and wrist color threats, which is seemingly silly but oh so stressful in the land of Remuda. In good time, I pray it will all work out; it will all be okay. It's just scary and frightening still. I know this is the raw truth of recovering.

My therapist told me I need to keep challenging myself. If I gain 5-10 pounds, what will that mean, he asked? To me, I said, it would mean I would not be thin, which would mean I'm not in control. He suggested I make "truth cards," which affirm how much John and my parents will continue to love me regardless of weight. I am worthy of that kind of love. I am worthy.

I'm not sure if it's just in my head (yes, it was just in my head), but I slowly feel bigger, like I have a fat roll and my belly is rounder. What does this mean in another 3 ½ weeks? I don't know. I am so scared. I know, though, that to overcome ED, I need to completely surrender. I am not ashamed of my struggle. No reason to feel guilt.

I think I'll head outside and read a bit before chapel. They FINALLY approved The Shack for me. Technically, I'm on transport (shhhh!) because I haven't been taking all my supplements. If they catch me walking outside, tough shit. Enough is enough.

November 9, 2010, Day #20

Today will be a good day. I'm not going to get down. I'm going to push through and enjoy art therapy with mom and dad. I will continue my journey and embrace what I learn.

Art therapy was certainly an emotional ride. Dad opened up and I never realized how MUCH my eating disorder may have personally affected two people I loved the very most. I caused worry and pain on my lowest days, when I just wanted to die and give up because my mind was starving, my body was falling apart, and the chemicals in my brain were all out of whack. They talked about how they worried if I would make it or not. I felt extreme guilt and shame, the tears flowing and heart aching, knowing that I may have contributed to my dad's heart problem and stint or my mom's consistent worrying. But, I must remember, the eating disorder may have caused this, but I did not. The eating disorder is NOT me. It is a disorder that overtakes my mind and body. Now I am reminded that ED does not just affect me, but all my loved ones. This will, I know, act as an extreme motivator to continue my recovery. Life is so much more than my body, so much more than calories, exercising, purging, bingeing, restricting and obsessing to the point of an all-encompassing eating disorder. It will not control me anymore. It will not live in all of my bones, destroying my body image, my confidence, my will and my capabilities in life. As dad said, I'm a capable being and the disorder has

NO place to steal that away from me. Mom loves me "to the moon and back". I love her more.

November 10, 2010, Day #21

It's another day of Family Week and another day closer to recovery and closer to going home. I broke down today when I was told to drink supplement at 2:30 p.m. snack, and I was again stressed at dinner when the girl leaving talked about how her jeans no longer fit. That freaks me out more than anything. If I get heavier here, where does that take me when I arrive back to the hustle and bustle of "fashionistas" in Columbus, intense work schedules and running. My psychiatrist here told me he suggests staying away from marathons for a long time. This is tough to swallow, as it has been part of my identity for quite some time. I miss it terribly, but at the same time, I haven't missed feeling like every run had to be a chore – a rushed and scheduled calorie-burning session to easy my anxieties about eating. It's a scary thought to think that running may be at the root of my eating disorder. Maybe running was a precursor, a result, or both, in all actuality.

Mom, dad and I will be doing the "Truth in Love" session tomorrow morning. This is a session of truth surrounded in love, in regards to the eating disorder, facilitated by my therapist. It will undoubtedly be emotionally draining, but good, all in the same. My stomach hurts right now and I feel like checking out of this joint! If I were to leave right now, I know I'd certainly be much better off than when I first got here. I'd be more in control, more focused and available to succeed with everything other than ED.

November 11, 2010, Day #22

Today was the "Truth in Love" session. It was amazing, cleansing. I learned the power of love. I learned I need to quit masking my anger with a smile. I need to express my individuality, find who I am and learn to love myself for it. My therapist enacted ED for me and I was to yell and scream and tell him to get out of my life. It was in front of a roomful of people. It was horrifying and I couldn't fully do it.

I'll take from this session the comments about my true beauty. It means a lot to hear that – that I am beautiful just for being me. Dad said I am most beautiful on the inside. Mom apologized for not getting me professional help sooner and for being a rigid and scheduled person herself. Dad apologized for pushing me too hard. I apologized for being heavy on their hearts, for causing worry when I ran marathons, determined to excel and burn excess calories despite my eating disorder.

We have always been open and honest about the eating disorder, so no huge revelations. My family is everything. Not the root of my eating disorder, they are my biggest supporters. It was cleansing and amazing to talk through the past six years.

November 12, 2010, Day #23

Oh. My. Gosh. I get to see Mr. John in ½ hour. He will be dropping off my parents at the last day of seminars (which he isn't allowed to attend...don't get me started on that one...you have to be engaged to be considered a part of the Family Week). I will be able to see him for five minutes, which will make my day. Later, he'll be able to attend the wrap up session and watch the rodeo, which I'm not sure if I'll be riding. I'd love to, but I guess it's my fault for not rapidly gaining weight or something. **Frustration.**

My dietician said I need a reality check. She said I haven't gained anything since coming to Remuda and she needs me to take ALL supplements in addition to more snacks. Right. Not Happening. (ED TALKING). I'm okay with my body, but I don't believe I need to gain, especially if I'm the same weight as I was upon admission. I wasn't underweight then and I'm not underweight now. I trust the dietician. She asked me if I thought she was lying. I don't think she's lying, but it's tough to stomach being forced to gain immediately. I want ED out of my life by eating food and loving the way my body naturally adapts, not by shoving fat shakes down my throat to purposely gain pounds. I've never naturally been past a certain weight, and I still don't understand why the dietician insists that I'm not at a healthy weight. To me, I am well on my way...and it's frustrating to not be anything but punished for my hard work.

Last night was more than I could ever ask for. We had to watch the rodeo because I'm still on yellow, but I really couldn't have asked for more, because this just meant I got to sit with Mr. John for an extra ½ hour. Afterward, we walked upstairs to check out for a "shortened" pass, and we saw a little lizard. John snapped a picture. The girls were hilarious and treating John like a piece of meat. We haven't seen the male species for weeks on end! They won't stop telling me how hot he is. Of course, I agree.

Dad fell on the steps. Go figure. I get my klutziness from him. He twisted his arm and scrapped his knee but promised he was fine. We went to the grocery and got fresh peppers, mushrooms, pineapple, red onion, shrimp, lemon and beef. John chopped them all up and grated the lemon overtop. Dad grilled and we sat around the table, prayed and ate together. I was COMFORTABLE. What a blessing. The biggest blessing? Seeing dad kiss mom. This week has brought us all closer. From the bad, comes good.

John dropped me back off at the ranch. I didn't want to say goodbye so soon. BUT I get to see them again tomorrow.

November 13, 2010, Day #24

Today was a day spent with mom, dad and John. My best day here. Enough said.

Sunday, November 14, 2010, Day #25

So, like I said, yesterday was my best day yet. I was in heaven because Meggie is starting to come back. I was able to spend the day with three people that I love the most. We started the day at the Hasayampa River Preserve and hiked around, even up a mountain (which definitely was against my "no exercise" rule...oh well!), and snapped some great photos on John's phone. Mom had flip flops on so was hanging onto John the whole way back down. So cute. Then, we ventured to Target. I got some socks, footies, and a sweatshirt and shorts. John got some moccasins and a coke zero (I stole a sip...or ten...ahhhhhh, heaven)! Since being at Remuda any diet sodas were strictly off limits, as was chewing gum. We went to Barnes and Noble and John talked to the "Nook" guy for about ½ hour – such a techy boy! He bought <u>Wicked</u> and my dad got us <u>The Girl with the Dragon Tattoo</u> to read. Next we went to Buffalo Wild Wings and enjoyed lunch and the buckeyes game. The guys stayed and drank beer (go figure) while mom and I snuck out to Super Cuts to get a trim and my eyebrows waxed. I felt like a woman again. I had to be back in time for dinner (boo. Hiss) because of my incompliance with the supplements, but I was more than satisfied with the day. John and I even started talking about moving in with each other in the near future. I'm comfortable with the idea.

Fran just braided my hair and I made a fall leaf bracelet for craft. I sometimes feel as though I'm back in kindergarten here, but that's okay. And, I know now, that's the point. I'm allowed to let go, just be. I will set my goal at the community meeting next, which will likely be to stop masking my emotion with a smile and to work on my body image. I'm still most scared of the fat shakes (supplements), but the rest of the day, I'm acclimated to the routine and able to get through the hours.

John, mom and dad came around 10 a.m. today. We were able to peruse around downtown Wickenburg, AZ, and stop in a cute shop. We also went to a little farmer's market and dad bought some jalapeno bread. John bought some apple butter. I was able to sit on a bench in the sunshine with Mr. John. With the sun on my face, John's arm around me, and a moment of silence, I was in utter bliss, if even for just a moment. A feeling of emotional fullness, stability and LIFE took over my being. WOW.

John liked my hair braided and said I needed to do that more often. The psychiatrist this morning said she could tell I was changing. My whole demeanor was calmer. I was more comfortable. When I saw my reflection in the store front windows today, I cannot say I was happy with what I saw; however, I can say that I am more accepting.

I'm starting the book Goodbye Ed, Hello Me, by Jenni Schaefer. I want to model her strength and courage of unveiling her eating disorder to those struggling. If you're reading this book, I'm so glad to have made a step toward this goal. Fully recovered, she makes great strides in two books and has become a renowned speaker. Perhaps, one day, I too can do this.

I called John later last night to make sure they arrived safely home. They did. I didn't get to chat much, but just felt content before bed, knowing they are all back, safe and sound.

Intermittent Optimism...{little rays of sunshine that got me through the anxiety, panic and worry while stuck in an inpatient facility...}

Words of encouragement and truth affirmation cards were big at Remuda. Gentle reminders of why I should love my self, day in and day out, once I returned to the inevitable real-world. Yes, treating oneself with proper nourishment and rest, potently focusing on emotional health was consistently practiced while in the bubble of Remuda, but what about once I got out? Would I really read my truth affirmation cards and remember that I needed to "love myself". Not necessarily. But, alas, I still created them in hopes of having these words somewhat engrained on my mind, a part of my being. I imagined hanging a few around my room, placing them delicately in my desk drawer at work and under my car visor. Though I never actually carried through on that, in fear of someone finding them and thinking I was A.) a weirdo with some neurotic tendencies or B.) quite narcissistic, I still benefitted from taking the time to use creative energy directly for myself. Simply taking time to think about me and the positives in life that God had so graciously granted and that simply couldn't be ignored any further.

A yellow index card read "Make my purpose to know and enjoy God...to be FILLED UP with him."

A pink one, "Acceptance and self love enable us to Grow and Change." Another yellow card, "Choose RECOVERY and LIFE." Finally a green one, "Choose to accept and love myself JUST THE WAY I AM." Others read as listed below:

Sit with anxiety. Don't react on it.

Choose to leave the driving to God. Give everything over. Release it all to Him.

Choose to stay in the GRAY. (a particularly challenging word of advice for me, with an intense tendency to stay in the all or nothing, the black or white).

It's my job to stay connected to God. His job is to do the healing and changing.

Act on truth, not emotions.

Recognize there are positive and healthy ways I can take control.

I choose to give myself GRACE.

I can't but God can. I'll let him.

I deserve to take time to nurture and enjoy myself every day.

Build your life around recovery, not recovery around your life.

Be still. Wait for the Lord. Take time to listen to him. PS. 37:3

Breathe. Slow down. Easy does it. One thing at a time. One bite at a time.

Live gently.

Stay in the moment.

Practice doing NOTHING. It's okay to just BE.

Enjoy my family. Celebrate them.

I deserve to take care of myself. Without caring for myself, I can't care for others properly.

I choose to leave the driving to God. I choose to thank and praise God. Give everything over to Him.

Stay focused on my recovery. Build my life around it.

I do not need to be perfect. That's unrealistic and impossible. Be IMPERFECT. It makes me, ME.

I choose not to wallow in the shame. I choose to give myself grace.

I deserve to get out of my head and into the moment. Practice presence. Live gently.

I need to let go. I need to let God.

I deserve acceptance and self love. It enables me to GROW.

Be strong and courageous. Do not be terrified; do not be discouraged, for the Lord your God will be with you wherever you go." Joshua 1:9.

I choose to love myself. I am amazing in God's creation.

I am worthy of a healthy weight to ensure my ability to reproduce.

I am worthy of indulgence.

I am worthy of nourishment, of health and nutrition.

I am wonderfully and fearfully made in God's image.

Physically:

I have beautiful, long eyelashes. I have strong, muscular legs that have carried me through many races.

I have my dad's ears and the "Feran" nose. I have hairy arms, just like my sister, Lynn!

Body image therapy was my favorite. Thursday mornings entailed the group therapy portion and periodically I would get one-on-one sessions with the body image therapist, Mindy. What an angel she was – confident and purely honest. A strong woman with a heart of gold and a passion to pass along her strength to those struggling with body image, low self-esteem and lack of self love. An average size and shape, she was beautiful in God's image; something many of us strived to be and strived to reach that level of security and confidence in our bodies. She posed us with two striking questions one day, 1.) Do you want to be skinny or do you want to be free? 2.) Do you want to have control or do you want to be healed? And those two questions hit home; they hit home hard. Another quote taken away from Miss Mindy? "And the day will come when the pain of staying the same will outweigh the fear of changing." Another day, Mindy began class by having us shout out characteristics of healthy communication. We came up with the following attributes: open, honest, receptive, respectful, non-judgmental, respecting of boundaries and the freedom to disagree and have own opinion. In applying this concept of communication, we were then asked to openly and honestly communicate with our bodies. Our bodies and our minds were two separate entities. My body versus my eating disordered mind and demands it put upon me physically. We were asked to write a letter to our bodies and then write what our bodies would respond. Please note this exercise was done three days prior to my discharge, having already spent 42 days at Remuda.

Here's what I produced:

Dear Body,

You are flourishing with health as you near your finish line at Remuda. You are again vivacious with shiny hair and bright eyes. Your bones are strong and your brain is back in order. ED has infested you for what seems like forever, filling you with fat lies and fat images. Outlining your reflection with swollen cheeks, thick thighs and a large rear end, bags under your bloodshot eyes and a belly roll and muffin top no matter how much food was deprived. Shriveled spirit and senseless soul, you were the target of an endless cycle of self-hatred.

Body, what I now hope for you is acceptance, love and maintenance by your owner. Sufficient fuel for a brand new car, one ready to embrace life fully, I will not neglect you. Vitamins, minerals, protein and vegetables -

strength provided to the image created in God. A beautiful smile, long eyelashes and a strong backbone, glorifying myself, my body which holds my heart, my soul. I'm sorely sorry for the mutilation, the abuse and hatred. Body, you deserve more than that and that's what you're going to receive.

And, my body's responding letter...

Dear Meggie,
You are right. You are now flourishing because I've been fed appropriately and given a proper six week rest from running. I was burning to the ground, fizzling out and frustrated. Running on empty and shutting to starvation mode as you ran marathons and neglected the signs I gave you. I almost gave up, shut down a few times when my limits were crossed, but I gave a good fight. I knew you would come around.

I don't trust you. No, not yet. I am full of life but scared to death, quite literally, of your old habits. I am terrified, actually, that neglect with creep into my crevices once again. Priorities of work and school, others before me - will I be put on the back burner again in no time at all? Please tell me no. I'm beautiful and capable, just let me be natural and free of these chains.

Love,
Your Body.
P.S. I'll regain trust with time and consistency.

While we're at it, sharing letters, below is the letter that I wrote to my running shoes. The dietician thought I needed to do this. I remember it being extremely painful to write, and I cannot say I ever actually accepted it.

Dear Mizuno Inspires,

With mourning and lots of sadness...I write to let you know you'll be sitting in the closet for a bit.

No more long strides on the sunny trails of Columbus and no more sprinting and competing on race days. This, however, is just a little hiatus, a bump in the road until your owner rebounds.

Nourishment, rest, recovery and rebuilding of the body, mind, spirit and soul after endless days of pounding will certainly result in renewed passion of our runs together. I could tell you were tired, too. Not so spunky, a little worn down and not such a spongy sole full of support. Not the joyous strides you once were the foundation of, but rather the constrictors of feet tired and weary of running the same route day after day, monotonously, robotically and regimented.

When I return, renewed and refreshed, you'll be laced for adventure, joyous and scenic voyages with plenty of energy and bounce in the step. Paced with perfection and armed with happy feet.

Hang in there. It won't be long.

Meggie

More Positivity: The Mailroom

Mail time was my favorite part of everyday. In fact, I dreaded the weekends – not only because they were painfully slow without programming – but mostly because we didn't receive snail mail. Not once was I allowed to check Facebook, to text, to call other than my 30-minute allotted time slot on the landline at Remuda; therefore, human communication through letters – a thing of the past – became quite important. The encouragement and words of love that follow from friends and family alike – whose names will remain anonymous for confidentiality reasons (except for my immediate family and boyfriend, John) – were what kept me sane. They kept me from giving up and provided a little light each day (except Saturdays and Sundays) toward the end of the tunnel – destination home and healthy. In no particular order, here are some of my favorites, about 20 or so...letters I'll cherish for years to come. On the hard days, I look back at them and smile. They keep me going. I have so many people for whom to live.

The first letter was actually written the day before I went to Remuda. My parents, I'll tell you what, they are the best.

October 20, 2010 (one day prior to my departure)
Hi Meg,

I wanted to get a quick note off to you right away, so you don't have to wait too long. I don't know how many days mail takes from Cleveland to Phoenix.

By the time you get this you will be settled in and on your way to recovery and healing. This is the answer to our prayers. It has been an emotional whirlwind these last couple of days, but I know you are in the right place. I love you so much – sometimes I feel like my heart actually swells up with all the love in it. I will write to you often – care packages too. I have enclosed a phone card. Will pick more up at Marcs (my mom's favorite store!) on Friday and get them to you.

Keep positive. You have a ton of support and love.

Love you to the moon,
Mom
XoXo

P.S. how do you like the Pisces paper? (the stationary she wrote on with her horoscope sign). Very old – when astrology was the thing! It's been a long time since I've written letters – maybe band camp!

Magpie (oh my dad and his nicknames...),
We love you and support you. You <u>will</u> get better. Someday you and John will have 3 (I want 4!) beautiful children and your problem will be a thing of the past. Be strong. You're a Feran. Love, Pops

Letter 1:
Always remember...you are ever growing, ever changing and ever becoming a more true and beautiful you.

Meggie,
Hey girl! How are you? I'm so sorry this has taken so long for me to write. Not an hour has gone by that I haven't thought about you! I hope you are doing well. I love you! Not too much to report in my world [...] I'm so excited for you to come home. I finished that class this quarter with a B! I've had to go to the coffee shop alone, but I thought of you every time. As I said I wanted to write you earlier, but I got no news [...]. Be well and I can't wait to see your face and hopefully you will want to go to Burger King with me! Love you.

Letter2:
Meggie!
I am so sorry it has taken me this long to write you.

I didn't know the address or if I was allowed to talk to you. I am so proud of you for going through with this. You are such a strong person and honest. I think about you every day and can't wait for you to come home. I hope you can still be friends with me – I will try to be less negative about myself too. It's not worth it, and I'm so ready to move on to bigger and better things. A number on the scale is not worth health, friendships, future family. I love you so much and you are so beautiful inside and out. It's your personality that shines and makes everyone love you – not your pant size. I miss you so much.

Letter3:
Hi Sweetheart,
I'm so glad you had your family and John for a visit. I know it is lonely for you being away from all that is familiar, but I am so proud of you and I pray you will know without a doubt that you are beautiful and lovely. I used to think that words described the physical, but they don't. The outward appearance can change in a heartbeat through many causes, but the inward is what God sees. To me, what God sees and is pleased with is all that's important. When we are OK with Him, He will take care of the rest. I'll write more later.

Letter4:
Hi Meggie!
I can't believe how long you've been gone. The time
has flown by! I'm glad it's ending soon because I
miss you tons. It's been so strange not having you
around! I hope everything is going well with you
[..]. Let's get a drink as soon as you get back!
Ok...maybe a few days after so you can catch up on
life. I bet Gracie and Brutus are missing you tons!

I hope you are feeling well and doing well and that
the time away has been everything you needed it
to be. Please know that I am here for you if you
need anything. Work would totally suck without
you, so I'm glad I'll be seeing you soon!

Letter5:
Hi Meg,
Sorry it took me forever to send this! One last card
before you get to come home. J I'm excited to see
you and of course I will eat breakfast with you,
help you grocery shop and go out on a double
dinner date! Please give this calling card to one of
the girls, since you won't need it anymore!
Love you.
Lynn (sister who I live with and am closest in age)

Letter6:
Meg,

I was so excited to get a card back from you, mostly because to me it meant you were doing ok. I'm sure you are dealing with so much there; I'm proud of you for being so strong. Please don't feel bad for not sharing this (the eating disorder) with me sooner. I'm happy you shared it with me at all and now I can be here to help you through your recovery any way I possibly can. Hopefully things are or will be getting easier for you! You aren't missing too much on my end. Just working and maintaining the house. People always said "wait 'til you get a house, then there's always something to do.' It is so true! If it's not the inside, then it's the outside. I spent three hours last Saturday just getting my yard ready for winter. I love my house, though, it's all worth it, especially when I put my x-mas tree decorations and outside lights up! Christmas is not far away and you'll be home before you know it. We're supposed to get our first real big snow the day after Thanksgiving...yikes! I'm so lucky to have you as a best friend. Don't know what I'd do without you! You are special – I love you so much!

Letter7:
See you in a few days. Let's go party!
Pops

I miss you a gazillion!! I can't wait to see you and hug you next week. This is going to be the best Christmas ever.
Love, Mom XOXO

Letter8:
A note from some relatives who sat around the Thanksgiving table without me that year. As I struggled to get through the heavy lunch of turkey, mashed potatoes and gravy and cranberry sauce . . . I didn't have the family to share joy and love. I was rather faced with other depressed anorexics and bulimics forced to eat a huge meal in the middle of the day. This letter, though, made my heart smile and the day just a little bit lighter.

Hi Meggie,
You are almost there! I am excited to have you home. It will be a Merry Christmas with you home and healthy. I love you.
Diane

Hi Meggie,
You are very strong. You have a wonderful future ahead of you. I am so proud of you. You are full of courage and fortitude. We miss you and look

forward to having fun this December saying "Baaaaaad" and "Thank you."
Lee (my brother-in-law)

Hi Meggie,
I am blessed with the best nieces and nephews! On Thanksgiving I thank God for His gifts. You are so special to me. Keep your eyes on Jesus. He will help you all the way. See you soon. Lots of love.
Aunt Rae

Hi Meg!
We miss you today, but this time away will be completely worth it when you are back home and happy and healthy. See you soon. Xoxo.
Lynn

Meg,
I missed you so much today, but knowing you are coming home soon and healed helped to get me through it. This is going to be the best Christmas ever! To the moon...Love....XOXO
Mom

Magpie,
Let's go to Wal-Mart, Target and Pattersons! It's time to move on.
Dad

Letter9&10:
My cherished love letters from my one and only!
(Disclaimer: Sorry, John, for exposing your gushy
and sentimental side...LOVE YOU!)

Meg,
So this past week was a little hard without you...ok
real hard, but in the end everything will work out. I
know I'm the luckiest guy there is to be with you
and I know this will work out to be an amazing
relationship for a long time. So what' new...let's
see. I haven't bought a car yet but might by next
Friday. I applied for a few jobs, so we'll see. Oh, and
I MISS YOU. Anyways, I can't wait to come see you
in about 10 days. Ok, I just have to say I LOVE YOU
dearly and am 100% your and will continue to be
yours. It's not changing. You are everything I have
ever wanted, period. Stay strong. You are more
amazing than you think.
Love you,
John
XOXO

Meggie,
Hey hun. I thought I would type you up a little note
while on break at work. I miss you dearly...like so
freaking bad. Yesterday was hands down the
hardest day for me. I'm doing better now but
yesterday was just horrible. I missed you so very

much – even more than normal – and just moped around, sat around, did nothing and felt horrible. Today has been a little bit better, but man, I almost lost it last night.

Babe, I hope you really know how proud I am of you and all the hard work you are putting forward. You're truly a strong and beautiful woman, and I am hands down the luckiest guy to be with someone like you. You make me a better person each day by being an amazing one yourself.

Words that describe my Meggie (please don't judge my lack of vocabulary):
Smart, caring, loving, beautiful, funny, strong, amazing, determined, gorgeous, spontaneous, outgoing, sexy, intelligent, organized (I know that's a weird one, but you always help me with it), always smells SO good (again, sorry it's on the list, but I love the way you smell. It's like a drug), motivated, and, most importantly, Meggie is my girlfriend. LOL. Ok so, I'm a little tired and having fun with this letter. Just...I miss my girl. Oh, side note, I gave my mom <u>Wicked</u> to read and she is real excited. I'm ¼ done with <u>The Girl with the Dragon Tattoo</u>.

Anyhow, you're the best thing to ever happen to me, and I can't wait to see you. I love you, Babe. GO

BUCKS! BEAT MICHIGAN (sorry, I had to add it). I love you dearly.

Love always (my one true love),
John

Letter11:
Hi Meggie,
I just wanted to write you a note of encouragement. I have been thinking about you, and I'm sure what you are going through right now must be challenging. I'm not going to claim to understand how you feel, but I can tell you that everything will be okay if you have faith. I think the one thing that everyone forgot to tell us when we were growing up was that "life is hard". We will all have struggles of our own that affect us in many ways. What we need to know is that we can't take it personal. Bad things happen. It is how we respond to those things that matter. Ok, enough of Mr. Encouragement. ☺ Rise and Rise again until Lambs become Lions!

Letter 12:
Hi Sweetheart,
Gosh, I think of you so often. I know all about doing and pushing through hard things…different things, but still hard. I have no doubt you can do this and do it well. Just as God was beside me in my darkest time, He is there beside you, Meggie. I hope you

enjoy this little book as much as I am. It expresses thoughts and feelings I've had for years locked inside of me. It explains it all so well. So happy your family and your guy are there to see you. Will write more later.

Letter13:
Hi Meg,
This is a picture I took of the full moon on October 22 – the day after you left for Remuda. Every time I look at the moon at night, I know that you can see that same moon. You are really not that far away at all because you are in my heart always. Family Week was enlightening for me. I learned a lot about myself. I truly do love you to the moon and back and can't wait to hug you again. (*note to readers: the name of my book came from this letter).
Love,
Mom

Letter14:
Hi Meggie,
I hope things are going well for you and you are feeling better everyday. I'm sure it's difficult, but no large accomplishment is ever achieved without a struggle. I love you so much and have been praying for you everyday. I hope these leggings

work for you. I have the same ones from Target. (Actually, unfortunately, the leggings had a huge hole in the butt area and I didn't realize until after I had been walking around in them for a few hours at the ranch. Luckily my sweatshirt was long and I had an extra pair of pants in my cubby. My eating disorder told me that it was because I was gaining weight and I ripped the hole with all my cellulite. In actuality, the leggings were from Target and the seam was ripped before I even had them on)!!
Love,
Diane

Hi Meggie,
I am proud of your courage and fortitude.
Love,
Lee

Letter15:
Meg,
I just wanted to send you a little something to let you know that I'm thinking about you. I'm so glad that you had the courage to get help so you can be happy and healthy again. I'm sure this is a difficult step, just know that you will get through this and everyone that loves you is supporting you. I'm happy that you were comfortable enough to share this with me, I'm sure it wasn't easy. Please know that I'm not judging you – I'm only here to help! Thinking about you all the time. If there's anything

I can do, let me know. Have a happy day. I love you,
Meg.

Letter16:
October 27, 2010 (six days into my stay)
Meggie,
It is so wonderful to talk to you and hear in your
voice that you are on your way to recovery. (This
was after conversing about the big pile of macaroni
and cheese I had ingested at dinner and somehow
kept down without panicking). I can't wait to see
you and spend time with you. I am enclosing my
rock from church. I remember when Diane was
getting a cat scan when she had cancer. I held it in
my hand praying that the cancer had not spread.
Now if you ever feel like you need strength, you
can hold it in your hand. Hope you enjoy the care
package. I had fun putting it together.
Love,
Mom

Letter17:
"I know things are tough right now, but just
remember...every flower that ever bloomed had to
go through a whole lot of dirt to get there!"
Hi Meg, I hope this package brightens your day a
little. I just want to remind you of how proud we
are of you for taking this huge step toward getting
better.
I love you. XOXO, Lynn

Letter18:
Hi Meggie,
I hope things are going well for you at Remuda
Ranch. I pray every night that you get better. I love
you so much and I know you have the strength and
faith to recover. I miss you and am excited for you
to get back. We will have fun over Christmas time.
We have a lot of good times ahead of us to look
forward to! I love you!
Love, Diane

Hi Meggie,
Set a vision for yourself filled with positive
outcomes, thoughts and goals of what you want the
rest of your life to look like. You hold all of the
power to make all of the changes you need. All of
the support people hold a minor role in your
therapy. You, like you know you are, will be the
major force for change. You have all the strength
within you to make all necessary changes that you
need. Have faith in God and confidence in yourself.
We love you and find you to be a wonderful
person.
Sincerely,
Lee

One of the girls with whom I immediately
connected, unfortunately left one week after I
arrived. Her time of growing and change was

coming to a closure as my journey just began. She jump-started my voyage, though, and spent my first evenings easing me with cinnamon tea and bananagrams, a great game of distraction in times of distress, by the way! She, however, didn't forget about me once she left. She sent me a Saint Anthony charm for protection and the prayer that got her through daily while at Remuda:

O Holy Saint Anthony, gentlest of Saints, your love for God and charity for His creatures made you worthy when on earth to possess miraculous powers. Miracles waited on your word, which you were ever ready to speak for those in trouble or anxiety. Encouraged by this though, I implore you to obtain for me...[here mention your request].

The answer to my prayer may require a miracle; even so, you are the Saint of Miracles. O gentle and loving Saint Anthony, whose heart was ever full of human sympathy, whisper my petition into the ears of the sweet Infant Jesus, who loved to be folded in your arms, and the gratitude of my heart will ever be yours. Amen.

This particular friend has become a lifelong one. We periodically meet at Barnes & Noble for coffee and gossip as she lives but a few miles away from me – small world! She is a devout Catholic – in fact, she helped arrange for communion to be given to me every Tuesday while away. Her struggle and road toward recovery continually inspire me.

My boyfriend's mother has suffered with lupus for years and is no stranger to life challenges. She too sent me continuous letters of encouragement and cards with hopeful sayings, like this:
 "Sometimes we make life hard by trying to keep things from changing. Lord, help me remember that improvement comes through some self-rearranging." I'd be happy to call her my mother-in-law someday.

Finally, below is another snippet of optimism that I found on my best friend's blog upon my return home. Her father passed away from brain cancer (glioblastoma) while I was away at the inpatient center. I think it sums up everything.

"The most beautiful people we have known are those who have known defeat, known struggle, known loss, and have found their way out of the depths. These persons have an appreciation, a sensitivity, and an understanding of life that fills them with compassion, gentleness, and a deep loving concern. Beautiful people do not just happen."

-Elizabeth Kubler Ros

Why did I include these letters? Because, if you are suffering from an eating disorder, you must remember how many people LOVE you. You not only have to beat ED for your own sake, but also for your family, your friends. Use them as your motivation to kick its butt.

Now that we've had an interlude of inspiration and positivity, which undoubtedly got me through the toughest or tough days at Remuda, I'll return to the thoughts that were going through my head, some not so positive, but 100% raw and real, nonetheless.

Meggie's Journal (daily musings, continued)

November 15, 2010, Day #26

Back to the routine today and I'm feeling stressed and anxious. They started the day by telling me I was on the list for transport. I'm smart, though, and snuck my way out of that. I convinced them I was just on yellow. I'm guilty and shameful for this, but I don't want to be the center of attention when it comes to that. That's me. This morning's breakfast was rough- oatmeal, an orange and scrambled eggs. I was miserable eating the eggs and I now feel overly full. I'm frustrated that I'm punished for not taking every single supplement. I'm struggling.

Less than three weeks. I can do this. I am worth taking the time to get better. Today, I need to ask Dr. R if I can get a phone pass to call work and also to call my doctorate program to see about registering for classes for next semester. This is what I want and need – challenge. First, though, I must be healthy. The same goes for exercise. Excessive can no longer be in my vocabulary. Recovery should be the number one word in my vocabulary. I want health, I want kids and I want a good life with John. These damn supplements are the only thing getting in the way. I did drink the morning fat shake today, but enough is enough.

I played scattegories with the girls today for about an hour. Now, I'll read for a while until lunch (ugh!), and I have home group this afternoon followed by an appointment with Dr. R and chapel. Once I get to chapel, I'm always okay.

November 16, 2010, Day #27

Happy Tuesday. I like Tuesdays and Wednesdays because of the stretching class offered in the mornings. I have a cooking experiential this afternoon. They sometimes put things on my schedule and then retract them since my Family Week was bumped up so early. For example, they first put me at the privileged table (where no table monitors are present and you're trusted to eat your food), and then they decided I couldn't be trusted yet. Dr. R talked about how the lower the weight that I leave here, the higher the chance of relapse. My mind disagrees. If they purposely try to fatten me up, I know I will go to extremes when I leave here to lose it right away. I will restrict, over-exercise, and put myself right back into the arms of ED. I know myself.

I'm in a happy mood right now. A breakfast of berries, rice krispies and a blueberry muffin. It sounds like a lot, but I'm okay. I'm okay.

November 17, 2010, Day #28

Unbearable Lightness by Portia de Rossi, that's a book I'll need to read next. Perhaps mom can send it or rather I can ask for it for Christmas. It's a story about her struggle with anorexia. This morning we had stretch and today is the day I've been dreading. I have an appointment with the dietician at 11 a.m. I've been forcing myself to do one fat shake (supplement) per day, and that's my limit. It's a bit embarrassing to be on yellow, not able to ride the horses, especially as a 27-year-old adult, but I know if I go home at an uncomfortable weight that surpasses my heaviest point, I will undoubtedly over-exercise and restrict. If I go back how I am right now, I'll work on getting back to running, but I WILL eat throughout the day and remember simple hints. Like, that breakfast actually jumpstarts my metabolism and keeps me energized and focused to succeed with life, like getting a doctorate degree or excel at work.

Yesterday, we heard from a speaker, who is a writer here at Remuda, Donna. She is legally blind from a childhood incident, when a swing set fell upon her. Coming from a "cookie cutter," perfect family, her dad couldn't bear this disability, and he committed suicide one year later. Her sister eventually committed suicide, too, when she was 25. Donna was a stone cold atheist for 33 years, but she finally turned to God. She said she'd do anything for her sight to be regained EXCEPT give up God. That tells me how much God means in her life. We each will receive a copy of her book, Broken Image. Yesterday afternoon, we did a cooking experiential with pizza and salad. This was a challenge, to say the least, throwing off my expected peanut butter and jelly sandwich plan. We were also offered ice cream. The three in my group, were similar to me, anorexic with some purging and over exercising tendencies, so we passed on that. It was nice talking to another girl, Lila, at snack today. She totally relates to my feelings because she's also been through both the anorexic and bulimic cycles.

...n a little quote tonight before I head down
...k house (where all us girls sleep and
...s monitoring feeding tubes and making
...n't purging or exercising every two
...less to say, I haven't slept too well
s... ...).

"Y... ...hould not come from outward
ado... ...tead, it should be that of your inner
life, ... beauty of a gentle and quiet
spiri... ...ch is of great value in God's sight."

November 18, 2010, Day #29

Another day in the life of Remuda. I'm working on
my discharge meal plan and I have my body image
class this morning, which is my favorite class. I met
with the dietician yesterday and my frustration sky
rocketed. More to come about that later...maybe.
Let's just say I'll be doing things my way in the best
manner for me and my post Remuda life. Period.
No more people pleasing. I'm not going to worry
about what my dietician thinks.

Here are some quotes I gleaned from body image
class today:

"If your body could have changed your emotional
pain by now, it would have. This (ED) is not about
your body!"

"As long as you are looking to your body as either the problem or the solution to your pain, you are living in full-fledged denial."

"You are who you are for a reason. You're part of an intricate plan. You're precious and a perfect, unique design, called God's special woman or man. You look like you look for a reason. Our God made no mistake. He knit you together within the womb, you're just what he wanted to make."

I like those. Being told twice in the past two days that the treatment team is *very* concerned for me has stirred my emotions to the extreme. Dr. R, though, told me he will never lose hop for me. He's worried that I'll fall back into the same destructive behaviors and intense running. He is probably correct, and I'm scared too.

November 19, 2010, Day #30

I've been here over a month now. I just drank my chocolate ensure, so there! I will continue to do one per day for the next week. That is my goal; however, I am going to keep positive because I know what is right for me (that was mostly ED talking; what was really right was providing my body with all the nutrients recommended by the expert). I have the strength through the Lord and will continue to talk to him and confide in him as I struggle. I had a dream last night that I was going to be moved to red status. I will continue to pray, keep a light heart and keep a happier outlook. It's what I need to do; I need to keep my chin up and take steps forward. I know the treatment team is only trying to push me to my limits, but the discouraging words are by no means motivating. They are debilitating.

November 20, 2010, Day #31

This morning started with a nice defecation (haha)! We joke that pooping is an extreme source of joy around this place. Pretty pathetic what my life has become: eating controlled and monitored meals, acting like I'm in kindergarten, having nurses flush my own toilet so I don't purge, chugging fat shakes, playing apples to apples and finally surrendering to a sleepless night monitored by nurses by 8 p.m. Oh man.

Anyways, I had a berry and yogurt granola parfait this morning and a toasted English muffin with apple cinnamon jelly. The dietician is now making me do metabolic additions, i.e., extra calories like orange or apple juice and additional EQs (a very Remuda term) at snack time. Annoying. To maintain my current weight, she insists this is required. I'm still not convinced that she is not just trying to fatten, fatten, fatten me up.

I had a body image session yesterday and I guess I do have a distorted image of myself. I added an additional 20 pounds on my thigh and 70 pounds around my belly with my estimates. I know I'm a bit distorted, but I also know I'll never be thin enough (ED talking...still). A bit of a problem to think that I'm never going to be thin enough. I still need to rearrange this thought and keep working on my ability to love my body, my soul, my heart and myself for all that I am and all that I have to offer. I am feeling so fat today, though. I'm not sure how to change this feeling. I just wish I didn't feel or think this way anymore.

November 21, 2010, Day #32

Another Sunday and a very fitting one – it's been raining outside for the first time since I've been here. The girls are watching the movie *Elf* in the background and Becky and I are painting our nails to pass the time until our community meeting. We have chapel at 2 p.m., but other than that, today will be boring. I might work on some affirmation cards or laminate some inspirational bookmarks. I feel motivated to keep going but also uneasy and uncomfortable in my body. Once we reach Thursday, I feel I will see the light at the end of the tunnel. I don't want Dr. R to think I'm just coasting along though, passing the time and leading to an immediate relapse upon my release. It's simply not true.

I'm determined to keep chugging along, to keep a balanced and stable diet throughout the coming years. I want this. No more purging. No more over exercising. No more restricting. No more bingeing. What a mess! What a nightmare! I never want to go back to that. NEVER. When, or if, I hit a bump, I'll think of those awful days as motivation, giving myself grace and honor to keep pushing beyond what I ever thought possible: recovery.

November 22, 2010, Day #33

We have equine in about 20 minutes. You see horses have been known to help girls recover from eating disorders. Their kind, gentle demeanor is contagious. This is how Portia recovered. You should read her book!

I'm dreading them announcing that I'm on TRANSPORT and yellow. This means I can't ride the horses, as my punishment. I honestly don't even care anymore. Well, apparently, I do care, or else I wouldn't be consistently writing about it in here. It's just embarrassing and demeaning to be punished for my refusal to gain unnecessary weight (ED talking). I will suffer the consequences, because gaining weight and becoming even more uncomfortable with my body will lead to more restricting in the end. I have my family's support on this, somewhat, so at least I can have some comfort upon my return home. Just 13 days.

Mom's thoughts (continued)

11/4/2010

It has been a week since I last wrote. I was busy planning for Family Week. I had to make plane reservations. Things about planes have considerably changed since I last flew, when Diane was two years old! I used to book flights all the time when I worked at a place called Parker. Back then, you called the airline and talked to a ticket agent. This has been a learning experience- looking for everything on line, including, cars, lodging. It's a game to try and get the best prices. I hope I did everything right.

Anthony (my dad) and I are flying out of Columbus on Sunday, 11/7. John is coming out to join us that Thursday and we will fly back together on Sunday. 11/14. The rest of this week Anthony and I have been "winterizing". We planted 50 tulips and 50 crocuses, fertilized, etc. I also have been spending time figuring out the logistics for our luggage, with the liquid and weight regulations. September 11th changed the way we fly.

I spoke with M a couple of times. I'm very pleased with the progress she is making. She is eating three meals a day and snacks. She says she is having night sweats, which means her metabolism is waking up. She has done art therapy (where she made something for me) and groomed and rode a horse. When she calls, she doesn't have much privacy, but it is wonderful to talk to her. She is going to make it.

When I think of spending 45 days away from family, friends and John in unfamiliar surroundings, I can only imagine how hard this whole process must be. But M is strong and determined. She is a survivor. I can't wait to see her on Sunday. In one of our conversations, M gave me some more insight in how she fell into ED (her eating disorder).

She said she was exposed to it starting when she was 12. Two teammates in high school suffered from ED. M's suitemate at college had an ED. Two teammates in college had ED. M became desensitized to it. Also, with our family being health conscious, I am sure I will learn and understand more at Family Week.

11/5/2010

M called last night. She remembered that 11/4/10 was the anniversary of Grandpa Toad's death. She never, ever forgets special dates. She has a memory like a steel trap. She said she hoped her day would be good with Grandpa watching over her. The reason I mentioned about planting the flowers ("winterizing" our house) earlier, is because whenever I'm outside planting, I think of my mom. She LOVED her flowers and being outside. I definitely inherited her love for being outdoors and working in the dirt. I remember when I was about 12, she gave me a plot of land to plant seeds. I planted zinnias. I was so proud when that straight line of zinnias was in bloom. I remember letting Diane, Lynn and M do the same in our yard. Bottom line: our family defines us. We are who we are because of them. I'm so proud of my daughters and the beautiful, talented young women they have become. I did good!

I received a note from M today. She quoted Corinthians 6:19-20. "You must know that your body is a temple of the Holy Spirit, who is within-the Spirit you have received from God. You are not your own. You have been purchased, and at a price. So, glorify God in your body."

11/14/2010

I am on a plane flying back to Columbus, OH. So much has happened since I last wrote. The flight is three hours, so I have a lot of time to catch up. I'm proud of myself and Anthony. We actually got to and from Phoenix successfully (thanks most to Lynn and John). We got one trip under our belt, so now we may actually be able to do this on our own. Of course, we had some humorous moments.

In Columbus, we passed seats when we were onboarding. We felt like fish going upstream to get back to them. On the trip back, going through security was laughable. Anthony (M's dad) set the alarms off two times while going through security. The first time, it was his cell phone. The next time, they didn't know what it was. They asked him to check his pockets. He reaches in a pulls out a bunch of Tylenol. He was asked what the heck it was. Then he told them it might be his stents (had heart surgery recently). Finally, they figured out it was just his belt. We forgot to remove our jackets and shoes ahead of time. The trays were already halfway down the conveyor belt. So, Anthony's Crocs floated down the belt without a tray!

Family Week. Where do I start? What an incredible journey. Talk about a roller coaster of emotions: many tears and many smiles. The day we arrived (Sunday, November 11th), we went straight to Remuda to see M. She had visitation time with us from 1:30-4:30 p.m. We would have arrived on time, but a tanker had turned over in the road and we had a hard time finding the actual ranch.

It was amazing to see her. We went in the lodge and she introduced us to some of the girls. Then, we walked around and saw the horses. We met two of the girls whose families were also here for the week. At 4:30, Anthony and I headed back to check-in at the suite. It was very spacious and clean. Then we went to the grocery to pick up food (and beer). They specifically asked that there be no alcohol on the premises, but Anthony and no beer for a whole week, just wasn't going to work. So, we had them pack the beer in paper and we would just sneak it in each night. Then, we would deposit the empties back in the bag, put it in the trunk and dispose of them on our next trip to the grocery! Ahhhh- what devious minds. We were in bed by 9:30 p.m. that night. Exhausted.

11/15/2010

Monday morning we started our day off with orientation and setting goals we wished to accomplish this week. Then, as we did each morning, we went to chapel (M's favorite part of the day). The musician, Jay, opened each day in song and praise to God. He played guitar- the words were on a screen- and everyone sang along. Then, we saw a video about how Remuda got started. The CEO gave his life story and talked about why he started Remuda. His daughter had an ED when she was just 10 years old. The daughter is now completely recovered, and she would speak to us later in the week. Ray, the pastor for Chapel, spoke to us after that. Each speaker had their stories to tell, struggles to overcome. They each were able to overcome them when they opened their hearts to God. Ray's little girls was lost and only found much later, possibly by an angel. The woman who took her "under her wing" found her walking along a dark street. She took her to a gas station, where Ray and his wife later rushed toward having received the phone call. They never were able to find the woman to thank her. No one in their small town knew who she was.

The CEO of Remuda's daughter struggled when she lost twin boys at five months into her pregnancy. She was feeling deep pain and then one day she suddenly felt extreme joy. That is when she knew God was carrying her. She and her husband have since adopted two girls.

The last speaker we heard on Friday was a woman who works for Remuda. She had low self-esteem growing up because of physical traits. She had scoliosis surgery when she was 15. She was in a full body cast for 6 months. She was very self-conscious about the scars left behind. Also, she inherited a large nose from her Jewish father. She obsessed over it growing up. She wanted it fixed. She got married when she was 40, and now is happy and centered in God.

After chapel each day, we separated into our adult and adolescent groups. The adolescent group had two families and our adult group had four.

12/5/10

Over the next few days, we would come to know these families by sharing our stories – both joys and sorrows- more than we know even our closest friends and family. No secrets. Complete honesty. And, as a result, healing.

Monday's morning session was an intro to ED. We learned that ED is not about eating; it is an emotional disorder. At noon, the girls returned to the ranch, and in the afternoon session each family shared their story.

12/8/10

I remember crying as I talked to the other families about Meggie's battle with ED and how I believed with all of my heart that M had been granted a miracle from God after we attended Dr. N's healing service. The miracle was her being able to come to Remuda to begin her healing process. Meggie had tried to fix herself, but she knew in her heart she needed help. She was ready to put her life on hold so she could get the help she needed- so she could live the kind of life she deserves: HAPPY, HEALTHY and with JOHN (and their FOUR children).

The highlight on Tuesday was art therapy. We were all told to create a picture demonstrating our feelings and how our loved one's ED had affected us. We were given many art supplies and 30 minutes to create our pictures. Most of the men struggled with this assignment. Anthony really struggled! The therapist gave him an idea to spark his imagination, and he began drawing stick figures. Anthony is good with words. Art, not so much. Meggie will always remember that picture. It gave her a good laugh. She plans on framing all of ours.

Anthony's picture demonstrated (in stick figures) his feelings of sadness, depression, anxiety, and finally hope. He also drew a picture of a bull "shitting" with the words (in Latin) "Taurus fecus" because Ed is a "bull shit" disorder. Oh, Dad!

I drew a picture of a moon in the night sky with the words "I love you to the moon and back". M's ED has caused me much pain and anxiety, but it has also brought me closer to M. We shared so much. I do love her to the moon and back. M's picture (which, by the way, demonstrated the best artistic ability in the family) had two sides. The left side was dark – a storm- demonstrating her life with

ED. The right side was light- a bright sunshine- demonstrating hope and the future without ED. Each family showed their pictures and shared their thoughts. It was a therapeutic avenue to share some deep emotions we've all been feeling.

2/7/11

I have definitely taken a long break from writing in this journal. Holidays, birthday celebrations and preparing for our trip to Hilton Head put it on hold for a while, but I'm back. I have plenty of quiet time in Hilton Head, where I am able to think and reflect. There is so much more to write. I hope my memory serves me well.

One afternoon, during Family Week, the families had a session with the dietician. She talked about good food/bad food and that there is no distinction. A brownie will break down into nutrients our body needs, just like an apple. I had a hard time accepting that analogy. With my somewhat "excessive" healthy eating habits, this was hard for me to buy into. (Like mother, like daughter). It became a joke that my biggest challenge was going to be eating a donut.

The dietician, being the food police, was not M's favorite person while at Remuda. She definitely had the toughest job: trying to get women with ED to eat. M's biggest challenge was the supplement, which more times than not, she refused. She had to wear a yellow bracelet indicating her refusal. She also lost privileges- riding the horses and some of her free time with us. Her supplement was my donut! Other girls got their supplement through a feeding tube at night. M refused the feeding tube. I give M credit for handling it the way she did. The girls with the tubes didn't experience the real feeling of fullness, as with the supplement. Somehow I feel M fought the harder battle – making her stronger.

2/8/11

The next two days were "Truth in Love" sessions. "Truth in Love" is an extremely emotional, cleansing experience. It's putting it all out there – total and complete honest.

For comparison sake, I found all four of these young women to have similar characteristics. They were all extremely intelligent, high achievers and people pleasers. Cee Cee and her could pass for sisters.

Just a note about these sessions. They each took place in our meeting room – which was a very comfortable setting – like a large living room. Chairs were arranged in a circle for the family involved, all facing one another. The rest of the families sat in the chairs on the perimeter. The family counselor and individual therapist sat in the inner-circle with the family, acting as the facilitators. Speaking from my own experience, you don't even realize there are other people hearing you pour out your deepest feelings. You become so focused on what brought us to this point and what we can do to start the healing process.

2/14/11

Our session was on Thursday morning. It's 8 p.m. on Valentine 's Day and my head is a little fuzzy from having two pale ales at the Oyster Factory (mom!!!). I wanted to write about our Truth in Love session today, but I need my own space and quiet time to write. Today was a beautiful, sunny, warm day at the ocean. Anthony and I spent the day at the beach with our good friends. Then we had dinner at the Oyster Factory. Even though the entry today will not be long, I still wanted to write about a mother's love for a child and why M's healing is my healing, too.

A mother's love for a child is something you can't put into words. When you hear that baby's first cry and they lay her on your stomach, there is an immediate bond between mother and child. It's like no other feeling I've ever had. So when your child hurts, you hurt. When your child is happy, you are happy. Remuda Ranch gave us our happiness back. I truly love M to the moon and back, and I thank God every day for her recovery. Now, she too will one day be able to experience that pure joy of becoming a mother.

2/19/11

Like I said, M's "Truth in Love" session was on Thursday morning. The anticipation was worse than the actual session. It was in some regards an eye opener to things I never realized. Each person in our family was a piece of the puzzle. The whole experience at Remuda taught me a lot about myself. First of all, I am too regimented with food and my everyday life. For example, I never eat donuts, I only have pizza on Friday nights, and I clean the house every Saturday. My eating habits made it difficult for M she lived at home after college. She felt guilty eating anything other than "healthy" food. Growing up in our family, M always felt different because of her darker coloration. Both Diane and Lynn were blonde. Anthony always called her a Puerto Rican, or "PR". I did know how much this hurt her, and I tried to stop it to no avail. Anthony thought it was funny, and he never realized how much it hurt M. In truth, we all thought M was beautiful with her dark hair, eyes and olive skin. I told her often that when she was older, she would love her beautiful tab. She just saw it as being different- to the point that her cousin told her she was adopted, and she believed it. This was something I did not know, and it broke my heart. I will never forget the day M was born. Her hair was pure black. I loved it and always will. It shines like the sun. M is absolutely gorgeous. I wish she had known this growing up.

Being the third child and following in the footsteps of Diane and Lynn was also difficult for M. She always felt pressured to be the best, both academically and athletically. I think both Lynn and M felt they had to do whatever their oldest sister, Diane did. I look back and perhaps not realizing it, I should have encouraged them to follow their own path in live. M was determined not to go to the same college as her sisters. She ended up at the same college. Once again, she was the little Feran on campus. Living with Lynn the past two years has been the best place for M. The apartment while she was in grad school, living by herself, was not good. My anxiety was not as bad knowing M was with Lynn, and if she was having a bad day, her sister was there for her. It was hard on Lynn. It caused a lot of worry and concern. She gave up a lot of social events to stay with M when she was having a bad day. She left work early to make sure she was okay. She kept us informed so we knew she was okay. I am so glad Lynn was there for her for the most part (unless she got really frustrated with the situation). She was a good listener and lent a sympathetic ear. It was more difficult for M to talk to Diane about the ED. Diane looked at the situation from a medical standpoint and logic. There is no logic with ED. I think Diane was more concerned with how it was affecting her dad and my health. Both Diane and Lynn really didn't understand how M got an ED when they were all raised in the same, loving family.

November 23, 2010, Day #34

This morning's "in recovery" group was inspiring. We watched something called the Hoyt series in which a father pushed his disabled son through the finish line for various races and triathlons. He had an amazing spirit and an amazing heart. The video certainly put things in perspective in terms of mind over matter. Also, it reminded me of the passion – the _true_ passion- that I have for running. I know it and I feel it. I get goose bumps running up and down my body every time I see the sport. It's an undeniable feeling, and no treatment team can convince me otherwise when it comes to that. I can listen and understand why running isn't a great idea in the midst of my recovery right now, but, realistically, I don't plan to give it up entirely. No marathons. Not seven days a week. Those guidelines, however, I can commit to.

We are decorating a Christmas tree right now. They try to make the treatment facility as "festive" as possible. For some reason, it's just not the same! I can't wait to get home and watch Christmas movies with John. I am very much looking forward to time with him – any and all time.

This morning my table monitor and BHT (behavioral health therapist), Susan, commented how perfectly and systematically I ate my yogurt parfait this morning. Next time, she said, I should stir it up! She made an analogy, then, saying I don't need to be perfect because God created me perfectly in his own image.

I'm surrendering more control to the dietician this week, allowing her to choose all my meals for me. Typically, we are allowed to select our meals using a monitor and have three choices per meal (all with the same caloric intake). I'm quite certain she'll know my fear foods, like pancakes and pizza. I'll have to suck it up, get over it, and just do it. I have to allow myself grace. As one of the girls put it, I just have to take it meal by meal so that day by day I get closer to being home and closer to being in John's arms.

November 24, 2010, Day #35

I just got back from equine and groomed a miniature horse, Wilma! She was so cute. Her son's name is Bam-Bam. She kicked back her leg while I was brushing her. It scared the crap out of me! I put conditioner in her tail and mane. I'll miss the horses and the smell of them (never thought I'd say that)! Tonight, I'll need to write a bunch of letters. My best friend from college wrote me one, which made my day. My Aunt Rae wrote, as did Diane and Lee. I talked to mom today and they were baking an apple pie for Thanksgiving. I'm bummed I'll be missing it tomorrow, stuck around a table with other anorexics and bulimics, stressing over the food. As Aunt Rae put it, next year I'll be back home and finally able to fully and truly enjoy the whole meal.

November 25, 2010, Day #36

Ten...days...left!!! Just ten days? I am starting to stand up for myself more. You'll never believe it! Last night, one of the girls was complaining how long it takes everyone to eat snack because they only open the rooms after 30 minutes of completion (to ensure no one purges). Another girl and I were the last in line- mind you there are 21 girls on our side- and literally sat down but for 5 minutes before she started bitching. So, I stood up for us and said it's hard when you're 15 minutes behind everyone else. Sounds like a small feat, but to me, it was a huge deal. I used my voice.

Also, yesterday, the dietician made a point to call me out and make me ride transport to her nutrition didactic. She singles me out and treats me like an imbecile, solely because I don't agree with her ideal weight and refuse to drink three fat shakes per day (looking back, I can't even imagine having her job). She doesn't compromise. She increased my snacks to 5-6 EQs and added metabolic additions, like orange juice and milk. I will be writing a patient concern form to her, expressing my frustration and hindrance on positivity due to her discouragement and restraints. So, happy thanksgiving to me. Awesome.

I had a blueberry muffin, cottage cheese and orange for breakfast. Compliments of my favorite dietician, a carton of 2% milk was on the side. I threw it away before the monitor saw. Sneaky.

November 26, 2010, Day #37

Moving on closer and closer and closer. Today, I openly expressed my frustration, annoyance and uneasiness in community home group. Man, it felt good, especially in front of the most infuriating person of all, the dietician. I put in a patient concern form to her and actually used my voice about how discouraged I have felt lately. My therapist has been giving me a cold shoulder, too. I guess it's time for me to leave? Have they given up? One more week, just one more week. This will be my mantra every time I feel sad or negativity begins to seep my brain.

I made a few Christmas cards and an angel. John must be so sick of getting my mail by now! I had a nice conversation with my boy last night and was even able to talk to his dad. He said he'd be sure to save a spot for me next year at the Thanksgiving table. It's nice to know they still respect me and have love for me, despite my eating disorder.

I have no idea what is in store for lunch today, as the dietician continues to choose them for me AND add metabolic additions, like 2% milk (woof!), hard boiled eggs, potato chips and sugar cookies. Infuriating. I have had it with her ever since she said I wouldn't recover unless I was willing to gain weight. A crock of crap, if you ask me (ED speaking). I believe I'm recovering by eating portioned, normal meals throughout the day.

November 27, 2010, Day #38

So, my therapist talked to my mom, John and Lynn yesterday. The negativity was shared. My therapist expressed how concerned he was for me. If I can't gain weight while in treatment, how would I once I returned home? Well, in actuality, I still don't believe that I need to. I've gotten over little mountains, but my treatment teams thinks there's still a lot that I'm holding on to and holding inside. So, it's disheartening and frustrating to think that they might be right. Apparently, John was given the dietician's number, too. He was told to call her and discuss me. I can only imagine what she'll say about me. Am I irreparable? Am I forever flawed? Is good never good enough? I believe in my ability to recover and continue down this road, but these negative surroundings are bringing me down. Down, down, down.

November 28, 2010, Day #39

My last Sunday here. It's a lazy, movie kind of day. I'm working on printing Bible verses to make bookmarks as Christmas presents. Also, I need to work on my discharge testing and write up some applicable notes about the book (assigned to me by my therapist) about perfectionism. I may actually use my room time (a privilege granted near the end of your stay, when you can go down to the bunkhouse individually, without a monitor). This will allow me to fold my laundry. I'm not sure what lunch and dinner may bring, as the dietician continues to choose my meals through tomorrow. I'll need to do my commitment letter for my promises toward recovery as I head back to Columbus, Ohio.

I talked to mom, dad and Lynn yesterday but I haven't yet called John. We had a little tiff because of the negativity the therapist told him. I'm still shooken up by his reaction, as he has been nothing short of supportive and full of positivity since my arrival at Remuda. One miserable conversation. I know he still believes in me.

November 29, 2010, Day #40

My last manic Monday here! This morning one of the girls passed out at the breakfast table. It's not an uncommon occurrence here. The dietician picked my breakfast, again, resulting in a blueberry scone. That was a challenge. Full of butter. Fat. I'm overly full and full of sugar. I'm shaky. It's okay.

Next, I have equine. I need to change into jeans and bring my camera down to snap some photos of Buster, Bobby, Wilma, Sundance and Scooter! This afternoon we have a life story in home group. We will have my "rock out" later in the week. Basically, I get a rock of hope and everyone says their goodbyes.

I'm still a bit bitter with my therapist today. He caused worry and concern within my family this weekend, saying that I'm not fully letting go of ED. I'm not so sure if it was a necessary ripple. I understand his concern and his desire for my support team to be aware when I arrive back home, but I'm tired of the pessimism. It's been like an entire Lenten season here. Just about 40 days. I am leaving a strong, determined and confident woman. It's strange but I'm beginning to distance myself from the girls, knowing the pain of saying goodbye. I need to get more addresses and pass around my affirmation book.

November 30, 2010, Day #41

I'm ready to blow this popsicle stand! This morning, I'll have "in recovery" group followed by a 1:1 with my therapist. I'm nervous to hear what he has to say to me. In the end, I know I'm walking toward recovery. No, I am not there yet, but I will get there.

Today, I feel bloated and gross. I'm not taking supplement at all anymore, but with the increased snacks and metabolic additions, my weight has remained stable enough that I'm not in danger. I came in here with the intention of losing weight. I was wrong.

Stretch this morning felt nice, and I can't wait to exercise again. I can't let the eating disordered thoughts drive the exercising, though. I am stronger both physically and mentally, equipped with the knowledge and determination to keep chugging along. I've made some lifelong friends through this journey. We've talked about having a

Remuda reunion one day. These girls truly understand me, like no one else. I love them.

December 1, 2010, Day #42

I'm upset and confused with a knot in the pit of my stomach. My best friend from back home just lost her father to cancer. And, I wasn't there for her.

Her dad fought a yearlong battle with cancer. The funeral is tomorrow. I feel sick over not being there for her. I just wish I could hug her right now. Wipe her tears. Hold her up.

December 2, 2010, Day #43

I just finished breakfast. I had cream of wheat, ham and berries. I feel full, but I feel okay. I am in a state of ease as I approach the Remuda finish line. I had a good last session with the dietician. She told me she was only hard on me because she cared. I knew that, deep down, all along. She told me she sees me as an amazing woman with so much potential. She thinks I still see myself as small and powerless, which is unfortunately somewhat true.

I was able to talk to my best friend from home last night. I'm praying for her. My mom took her family some homemade macaroni and cheese. The other girls will take care of her today. We all have an extremely special bond of friendship. This makes me again realize how unpredictable and senseless life can be. I will talk to God today, praying for her as hard as I can.

December 3, 2010, Day #44

What is it that makes you come alive?
Some brief discussion during my final spiritual 1:1 session today. The spiritual therapist said he can see the genuineness back in my smile. God has come back to my life. I will continue to nourish this relationship so it continues to flourish back home. With God's grace, worry fizzles. He knows all; He will take me on my journey, fearlessly and beautifully. I know this now. I trust in Him. Ease, comfort and peace have come over my spirit. I am God's beautiful princess and He loves me wholly, entirely, and completely.

I have a headache and achy limbs today. Saying goodbyes today has been emotional and bittersweet. I have an excited, yet mournful heart. Above all else, I am so happy that I get to see my family, friends, and my John so very soon.

As part of my goodbye, I presented a commitment letter to my treatment team. It's part of the program, and I think it helped me put into perspective what I'll need to focus upon to stay in recovery back home. I do not know if I will be able to perfectly follow everything I wrote, to be honest. But, I am shooting for these commitments. I will be okay, if I don't let ED break my promises. That's the funny thing, I'm such an honest and loyal person, but when ED takes over, I lie and manipulate, just to get out of eating. It makes me sick. It's not me.

Below is what I shared with the group on my last Friday at Remuda:

Commitment Letter
Meghan A. Feran

In the midst of a hellish cycle of restricting, then purging, then over-exercising and pushing myself until I collapsed, I knew I couldn't hold on much longer. I was losing myself. Meggie was slowly disappearing and losing her personality, her intelligence, her focus, her charisma and connection with others. ED had his claws in me and as each of the six years past, he seemed to dig deeper and deeper. Not only was he affecting my physical health, but all those around me were feeling a trickle effect. I was not the same. I was an emotional mess who would rather isolate then spend holidays with my loved ones, attend baby showers for my best friends, and go out for dinner with my soul mate.

ED kept feeding me empty promises, day after day after day. My once passion, running, became a robotically, monotonous chore. To burn calories and nothing more, I competed weekly and trained for consecutive marathons. A week before making the choice to come to Remuda, I ran my last marathon and came so close to passing out at mile 25. I felt extreme fatigue and dizziness. I had to walk for most of the last mile. My body was failing and God was there to catch me one last time. This was my wake-up call.

Though I haven't sailed smoothly through the program here at Remuda and admit my struggles along the way, I do know that I'm leaving a more confident, stable and strong woman, full of grace and determination to continue working toward recovery. Harder than I ever thought it would be to let go of ED, my motivation continues to stay. My hope for marrying John and raising a family together keeps me strong. I, Meghan Anne Feran, commit to the following on my journey toward complete recovery:

★   I commit to having regular appointments with my therapist, dietician and support group in Columbus.
★   I commit to staying away from competitive racing and Brooks' sponsorship for at least 3 months as the environment is not conducive to my recovery.

★ I commit to saying no at work and not overbooking my life to the point of burn out. I commit to working my 40 hours and then taking on extra, only as it fits with my recovery.

★ I commit to taking time for me, taking time to be still, relax and kick back without guilt at least ½ hour per day.

★ I commit to going to church weekly, trusting in God and finding a local bible study group to join.

★ I commit to following my discharge meal plan to start on the right track and continue a regimented and planned schedule for as long as my outpatient team deems necessary.

★ I commit to being open and honest with my sisters, mom, dad and John and admit any and all slip ups before sliding farther. I commit to reach out and not feel ashamed when I need a shoulder to lean on.

★ I commit to continue to express my emotions and show something other than a smile when I'm feeling frustration, hopelessness or pain.

★ I commit to hold myself accountable from over-exercising by first limiting the days and length of exercise and by joining the same gym as a friend so I don't go alone.

★ I commit to find another hobby besides running - whether it be learning the piano, knitting, scrapbooking or joining a book club.

★ I commit to continue to work on my body image, to accept myself for who I am and learn to love myself just as God loves me and created me in his image.

★ I commit to continue to read my affirmation cards and challenge negative body talk.

★ I commit to passionately raise awareness for eating disorders and make its declining existence a part of my being to the best of my ability.

★

December 4, 2010, Day #45

Whoa. My last day here. This morning, as I began to put on my make-up, my roomie told me I didn't need it and that I'd be just as pretty without it. It moments like these at Remuda that I'm going to miss. I just had a peanut butter and banana quesadilla for breakfast. It was delicious! I was always nervous to try it, but today I challenged myself, and, boy, I'm glad I did. We are watching the movie, *The Santa Clause,* my suggestion, of course. I love, love, love the holiday season. I start packing up today and I get to skip some programming! Today's breakfast was entertaining. My one roomie won't eat fruit. So, when the table monitor left for a quick second, one of the other girls grabbed it and guzzled it down quickly for her. We have each other's backs.

Right now, the girls are sitting, chatting, laughing and being goofy. I'll miss their smiles. I'll miss their support. I'll miss the comfort of being surrounded by others struggling with the exact same thing as me. Mom and dad will come visit me once I get back to Ohio. It will be nice to have their support as I re-enter reality those first couple of days. I have the best boyfriend, too. I will push through. I have strength, a clear mind and a light heart, armed with the power of God.

December 5, 2010 – Discharge Day

My roomie and I both discharged today. I woke up at 2 a.m. to send her off. We hugged. We cried. We began this journey together, and we ended this journey together. I remember the first night, being shoved in a room with this complete stranger. Waking up fearful and faint, malnourished and shaking, the forty-five days have transformed both of us. We leave strong. We leave determined. I was sent to catch my flight at around 9 a.m. It was surreal. Goodbye, Remuda. Thank you for taking me into your arms. Thank you for saving my life. Thank you for taking this burden off of my family.

I'd like to close with all the letters I wrote to my peers, who were going through the same experience and whom I had a connection to like no one else, the day before I departed Remuda. Perhaps, with a little luck, if this book gets published, each and every one of you will know, you helped me reach recovery, more than anything. Misery loves company, after all, and I couldn't have asked for better company. You all have a piece of my heart, always and forever. Thank you for saving me. I can only hope I helped save you.

Dearest B,

Hi doll. I'm so glad I got to share in part of this journey with you. You are one of the sweetest, most genuine people I have ever been in the presence of. I can see you want recovery and that makes my heart smile. I have been inspired by your willingness to accept being here and embracing whatever the day brings, no matter how hard it may be. I'm going to miss your hugs and sweet chats. I'm going to miss your cute, "fashionista" outfits and sweet laugh. You have this in you, B. I'll be praying for you. Remember that you're so worth this. You have a family that loves you, a future husband who will sweep you off your feet, just like you deserve. If I'm ever in the Colorado area, I'll be calling you. If you're ever in Ohio, please let me know. Keep in touch. I know God has amazing plans for you.

Dearest Z,

I'm so glad our paths crossed, even if just for a short time. I know God had a reason for us meeting, and I'm glad he did! I love your bubbly personality and cute stories. I love your zany spirit and "hippy dippy" ways. You make me laugh, and I love your smile. You have a lot to share and I'm so glad to see how you've used your voice in groups. Reach out when you need it, because YOU DESERVE IT. You are a beautiful woman, and you deserve to embrace and see this, just like everyone surrounding you does. Please keep in touch, my dear. I'll miss you.

AE,
I just wanted to say how happy I was to have met you; I know God had our paths cross for a reason. I've been inspired by your positive attitude all along and envious of your ability to comply and let go, to really trust in Remuda and beat stupid, old ED. I know you're going to be just fine because you have a strong stamina and spirit; determination seeps from you. Thanks for keeping things light around here – I always enjoyed your dancing and great sense of humor. Stay away from Mr. Buster the rest of your time here...no broken bones allowed. I hope you have an absolutely wonderful holiday season once you bust out of this place! I'll miss you. Please keep in touch. Remember to get the full-fat mocha the next time you're at Starbucks, just like we promised.

L,
My partner in crime...I absolutely adore YOU! I'm so glad we were able to cross one another's paths and I know I've made a lifelong friend in you. Keep on hanging in there, day by day, and you're going to be free with a CELL PHONE and SLEEPING IN in no time at all! Your light spirit and smile always made my day that much better. Thank gosh you came when you did...you seriously helped me get

157

through this more than you know! I'll never forget playing the chicken game with you (we totally sucked...hehe) and complaining about those damn ensures. ☺ But seriously, you rock. Thank you for being you. Please, please keep in touch, girlie! White water rafting, skiing or Vegas is calling our names!

F,
Where do I even begin? I love my little penguin. My professional hair-braider, my favorite giggle buddy, my great hugger and constant listener- I'm going to miss you more than words can express. I love your bubbliness...you are EFFERVESCENT. I honestly wouldn't have made it through this journey without your spirit, constant motivation, and words of encouragement. You are so mature and amazing. God has amazing plans for you. I can't wait until the boy of your dreams comes and sweeps you off your feet. YOU DESERVE IT. You better be calling me and telling me all the details, because I have a feeling it will happen sooner than you know it. Please promise me that you'll see what everyone around you sees in you – BEAUTY. You are so worth a wonderful, healthy, successful life full of love. The world wouldn't shine so brightly without you. I can't wait to run that half marathon with you...wink wink!!...and take that trip to NYC. You are AMAZING.

M,

Hi beautiful! I am sad that I didn't get to know you for longer than a week, but I can already tell you are an amazingly strong woman, determined to kick ED to the curb. I'm inspired by your ability to not only do this for yourself, but also for your family. I consider you a role model for your grace and strength to take that step toward health and happiness. I'll be praying for you and thinking of you often as you get through this recovery day by day – it's going to fly by! You are so worth this. You are beautiful.

E,

I just wanted to say goodbye...I'm not so good at goodbyes. Anyways, you are so worth this. You are a beautiful woman, wife and mother. Your family is blessed to have you. I love your spirit and your strength certainly shines through. Just remember that you are good with God and through him, all things will be okay. I'll be praying for you! Please keep in touch and let me know how you're doing. I'll be missing you dearly.

M,

It's been nice getting to know you and I've appreciated your solid spirit and sense of humor. I know this has been hard and it's not going to disappear overnight, but I also know you have the determination to kick ED to the curb. I've seen you grow over this journey and am so impressed by your maturity. I'll be praying for you and thinking of you often. If you ever need anything at all, please know you can call on me.

T,
Hi my Canadian friend! You are GORGEOUS. You have it in you to beat this horrid disorder and start living your life the way it was meant to be lived! I've loved chatting with you, playing games, harassing the nurses about getting us our darn coffee, and listening to your cute accent! Thanks for sharing this journey with me – you were always a comfort to me. Thanks for letting me in on the secret of LULU Lemon and Bench – I think I'll be doing some online shopping when I get home. I'll be thinking of you often. You deserve this. I'll miss you!

J,
Oh my little J. Where do I begin? You are the best, the absolute best. I couldn't have asked for a better roomie to get through all this together. You are such an amazingly caring soul, and though I know you'll disagree, I just wish you could see yourself as others see you. You deserve to love yourself, because you are everything lovable. I also know you are extremely intelligent and determined, so I know ED has no place in your life anymore. You

deserve to live your life the way it was meant to be lived – free of chains and self-denial. I'm going to miss you, girl. I have LOVED getting to know you, chatting at night and goofing off...trying to catch squirrels that burrowed in our walls. Let me know when you're in OHIO – you ALWAYS have a place to stay. I'd love to hear how you're doing.

A,

My long-lost roomie! I'm going to miss you. I feel like we've been through a lot together, through the drama of Remuda and the farts of Cooper...you have been a constant optimist and caring soul. You've helped me grow more than you know. I always appreciated your honesty and ability to lighten up situations and have some fun. You rock. You deserve this. ED has no place in your life. I'll be praying for you often. Please keep in touch – I'd love to hear how you're doing.

CK,

Coco! I have enjoyed getting to know you more and more each day. You are such a light in our group meetings – always contributing and bringing laughter and joy. I'm so blessed to have met you and am going to be praying for you often. You have endured so much and now it's time for you to live that life you were always meant to live, without ED hanging around. Believe in yourself. You are so worth this. You are a gorgeous woman, inside and out. I hope you can see this.

L,
I couldn't have done this without you, girl. Thank you for always giving me your smile when I needed it most, for listening to me vent, and for sharing in my obsession of late night tea ritual. You are the BOOOOOMB. I'm going to miss you so much. You've become like a little sister to me. I care about you like a sister, too. Please keep that determination and drive to abolish ED from your life. He has no place in it. Trust in God and everything else will fall into place. I'm going to miss you so much. I know I've made a lifelong friend in you though, and I have a feeling I'll be seeing you again. Me, you and L should have a mini reunion this summer....pretty please? LOVE YOU!

S,
PFFFFFFFTTTTTT. BEAWR! I LOVE YOU, ROOMIE! Though you've scarred me for life with the bathroom door incident, I can't thank you enough for all your encouragement along the way. You've been a saving grace to me more times than I can count over these 45 days. Thanks for listening and being such a caring soul. I love your laugh and love seeing you happy. ED has no place in our lives anymore. I'll be checking up on you. Text me!

Facebook me! We still need to plan that vodka and Ensure party. I'll miss your farts. NOT!

R,
Hey you! I've loved getting to know you and am so glad we were in the same group. I know I met you for a reason and I've appreciated having you here more than you know! Thanks for always smiling and always offering a kind, gentle spirit. I pray that you can see what a gorgeous soul you are, both outside and inside. Keep your determination up because you deserve to live life fully and healthfully – without ED. Keep in touch, girl.

CH,
You are such a blessing. I'm SO thankful that I got to spend the last week and a half or so with you here. I know God had our paths cross for a reason. You are an amazing woman - your determination and strength show through your smile and how you consistently reach out to all the other girls around here. My hope for you is that you take the time to take care of YOU, too. You are beautiful. You deserve to nurture and love your body, just as God does and has created you perfectly in his image. I'll be praying for you. You deserve to live your life fully and wholly – without the chains of ED anymore. Hang in there; it's all going to be so worth it.

A,

Hi beautiful lady! I am so glad that I got to spend some of this journey with you. Though Remuda has been incredibly tough and frustrating at times, I feel so blessed to have been surrounded by people like you through it all. I love your sense of humor and think you are absolutely gorgeous, both inside and out. I'm always amazed by your ability to use your voice and I pray that you can see how beautiful you are. I know your boy adores you and you are going to be just fine with that support and love. Please keep in touch, my dear, and let me know how you're doing.

AD,

I am so glad our paths crossed, even though it was at Remuda! I know God has amazing plans for you. You are a bright light, a beautiful soul, and an amazing woman with so much potential. Never sell yourself short. I know you are DONE with ED and can see your determination daily. I'll be praying for you and thinking of you often. Thanks for always being there for me – for the hugs and cuddles – it helped me more than you knew! Keep in touch and keep believing – you are SO WORTH THIS.

Mom (reflection after M's discharge from Remuda)

2-23-11

I'm sitting on a dock writing this. It's a huge tide, and I can't get to my normal chair where I do my best thinking. It's windy and the ocean is pretty riled up today, but ever since I read The Shack, I think of the wind as the Holy Spirit. Yesterday, I got a text on my phone. Early morning texts still make me worry. M did have a bad night with a lot of purging. But this has only been her third hiccup since returning from Remuda. We talked later in the morning, so I found out what triggered it. This week is National Eating Disorder Awareness (NEDA) week. M has signed up to be a speaker for NEDA. The first event is tonight, at Ohio State University, where she will speak about her experience with ED. She asked her boss if she could leave just a few minutes early to make it there in plenty of time. With good intentions, her boss asked M if she was ready to do something like that, being that she is still in recovery. It triggered a negative feeling in M, which weighed heavy on her the rest of the day. We had a good talk. When she has these set-backs, she is still very logical and knows it is a little hiccup. She will recover from it and continue to move forward. She does not get into a deep, dark hole anymore. She said she was going to pray to God on it. I told her to go with her gut and her heart. I am so proud of her and the courage it takes to do this. She is putting herself out there, but her goal is to help just one person. It didn't take her long to make her decision. She sent me an e-mail the next day, saying "I am strong and confident. I'm going ahead with the event at OSU."

Everything that Remuda instilled in her has stayed with her. I thank God every day for Remuda and her road to recovery. I know M is going to help someone with her courage to be real and to speak. You go girl!

2/24/11

Talked to M after her presentation last night. It was a positive experience for her. I knew it would be. God has a mission for M to help rid the world of ED. The girl who organized the presentation at OSU is doing her senior year thesis on ED. M cautioned her that her independent study in college, centering on the "Freshmen 15 Phenomenon," may have been a trigger toward obsessing over food. Another girl at the presentation approached M afterward. She had neared an ED in high school. She played basketball, and her coach was tough on her. Once again, that was one of the triggers that was brought up in M's "Truth in Love" session. M's high school coaches were tough- to the extreme. It was too much pressure. The coaches pushed them too hard physically and were verbally abusive. A boy also approached M and asked about men and eating disorders. He wondered if most didn't admit to it because of the whole masculine image thing. This is probably true. M wondered if perhaps he or someone he knew was struggling. After the presentation, she and John were meeting for dinner. She felt good today, both physically and mentally. Her hiccup was just that- a hiccup.

3/3/11

M went to a friend's housewarming party over the weekend. She has always kept her ED a secret, ashamed of it. Only one of her friends knew anything at all. When she left for Remuda, though, she felt it only right to tell a few more of her closest friends. She knew with the close contact they have through cell phones and Facebook ® (which she would no longer have access to either), that they might be concerned not hearing from her for 45 days. She felt she owed it to them to tell them. Her best friend's father died while she was at Remuda, and we knew there might be more questions why she wasn't there. She told me I could tell people if they asked. She didn't care if people knew anymore. She wanted to be honest. She has become more open about ED.

So this weekend, when she got together, she opened up about Remuda. They all took time to share their own demons. That is what a good friend is- someone you can share your deepest and darkest secrets with- knowing they will understand and not judge. M is blessed with wonderful friends.

I have gotten off track a little bit. There is more to tell about Remuda. But as some of these events happen, I want to write about them while they are still fresh in my mind.

One other thought before I go today. M was at Remuda for 45 days. I will have been gone for 41 days here in Hilton Head. Being away from home and friends is hard. There truly is "no place like home," no matter what the weather is. M wants to get back to Cleveland soon so she can be closer to her best friends, her support group.

8/7/11

Wow! Where has the time gone? Much has happened since I last wrote in March. We had a baby shower for Diane, a bridal shower for Lynn and a 70th birthday party for Anthony. Lots of changes in the family. Lots of planning for all these events. Lots of fun, but also very time consuming! It is a beautiful summer afternoon, and I am sitting in the backyard on a lounge chair writing this. The next big event will be Mollie's birth. Diane is due August 30th. Before things get crazy again, I'm going to attempt to finish this journal. I forgot to mention that both M and Lynn moved in July. M is in an apartment in northern Columbus. I know it's harder for M to live alone, but John is close by and they spend a lot of their evenings together. M still struggles with ED, but she also has a brand new attitude about it. She has a new therapist who is faith-based. I like that she is Christian based. This helped M a lot at Remuda Ranch. M has also found a church and is trying to attend on a regular basis.

M has been back to restricting and purging more. Her doctor put her on a higher dose of anti-depressants to see if that will help control the urges. M is still fighting the battle with ED, but she does NOT give up. John and her had a rough patch a bit ago, too. He was feeling frustrated with ED. They resolved it and are still in a very strong, committed relationship. John had a health scare this past week, too. He had some blood work done and the preliminary results indicated the possibility of a connective tissue disorder. When the results finally came back in negative, M said it felt like a 50 pound weight lifted off her chest. That kind of worry is what John feels for M. He needs her to be better.

I think another piece of the puzzle that will get M closer to complete recovery is MOLLIE. I think when Aunt Meggie sees that little baby, she will know in her heart that if she is going to be a mom, she will need to beat ED, once and for all.

John and M talk about having four children. When I see the love between them, I know they would make awesome parents. In May, they flew down to Hilton Head for four days for our family vacation. Seeing them together for that period of time, they just glow when they are together. M seemed to do really well with the eating when she was there. She seems to do well with ED when she is surrounded by love.

10/4/11

I'm back! My goal is to finish this journal before her one year anniversary at Remuda. Since my last entry, our little angel, Mollie, was born. She is a light in everyone's eyes. She makes your heart glow. M and Lynn were able to make it up to Cleveland for her birth. It was an amazing, memorable experience for all. We have had two more showers and a bachelorette party for Lynn. The pace is picking up now with only 18 days until Lynn's wedding! Diane goes back to work next week, so I expect my life to be a little crazy watching Mollie for a bit.

M left for Remuda last year on Thursday, October 21st. On October 22nd, there was a full moon. I took a picture of it and sent it to her. This year, there will be a full moon on October 11th. We have come full circle.

Now, before I move forward, let's skip back to a section of M's journey I haven't covered yet: John's visit. John's visit to Remuda was what helped M get through 45 days away from home in treatment. John flew into Phoenix on Thursday evening. Anthony and I co-piloted the trip to the airport. Driving in a large city at night was a challenge, but we made it. After we picked up John (and fired up his GPS system), we stopped at Burger King and then a gas station for some beer. John drove with us on Friday morning to drop us of at the session so he could see M before we began. John is JUST what M needed to see. Friday was only a morning session with parents, so John headed back to the condo and watched a DVD on ED. Friday afternoon and evening, M had time to spend with all of us. She decided rather than going out to dinner, we would shop and cook dinner together at the condo. She and John decided on shrimp and veggie kabobs. It was a wonderful evening. Anthony grilled the shrimp and pineapple. M and John worked together slicing the vegetables. We sat at the table to eat and played a game. M had to head back to Remuda by 7 p.m.

10/9/11

I talked to M this morning. She had a good night with John and a few friends, watching the Ohio State game. Okay, back to Remuda.

Saturday morning (of Family Week), Anthony, John and I spent the morning together at the condo. John goes to bed talking about sports and wakes up talking about sports! TV has also turned into sports. With Anthony and John, I was outnumbered. We picked up M early and went for a hike in a park we found. The scenery was beautiful. M's challenge was to eat lunch out at a restaurant. She chose Buffalo Wild Wings. We dropped Anthony and John off at the restaurant fist and M and I went to get her a haircut. Afterwards, we went back to meet up with Anthony and John. We all ordered and had a great time. M met the challenge.

10/10/11

My memory is a little foggy after a year, but I think after lunch we went back to Remuda for the horse show. M was not able to participate because she was still refusing her supplements.

10/13/11

Today is M's 28th birthday. A day to celebrate. I wonder if there was a full moon the day she was born, too. I talked to M this morning on her way to work. She is celebrating with John and Lynn tonight. On Saturday, Anthony, me, Diane, Lee, Lynn and Grant will celebrate with her at dinner. We are going to the Asian Bistro.

I love M so much, it makes my heart sing. Last year at this time, she didn't even know yet about the opportunity that would come from Remuda. She found out on the 19th and was on her way two days later. So much has happened since last year. Lynn and Grant's engagement. Mollie's birth. A new apartment. A new job. Life changes, and it comes at you fast. These are exciting times for all of us.

I'm watching Mollie today while Diane gets her hair done. She is squealing and cooing right now. There is no greater joy than being a mother. It takes a tremendous amount of patience, as Diane is learning. Being a new mother is very demanding, but it's worth every second for that child who you love to the very depth of your soul, forever. I teared up a little thinking about the joy Mollie brings to our lives. I want M to experience that joy.

M will take control of ED and banish him from her life, so she too can have a healthy baby with a healthy mom.

Back to Remuda – one last time. Sometime on Saturday, M's therapist met with all of us. We probably spent a half hour with him, including John. It was good that he was able to talk to John and explain some things to him. M also showed us around the grounds at Remuda. There was a large tree where all of the girls left rocks with messages around the base. She also showed us a climbing structure, which presented a challenge for the girls to face their fears.

10/14/11

On Sunday, we only had a half day to spend with M before departing. We filled it to the brim. We spent the day in the town of Wickenburg. We went to all the gift shops and took lots of pictures. Anthony bought a souvenir coffee mug, which he took to Hilton Head to enjoy his morning coffee. Unfortunately, it got dropped on the floor and broke. I need to find the name of that gift shop and get him another one. Along the streets in Wickenburg, they had many statues of donkeys, cowboys and cowgirls to pose with. It made for some cute pictures. We also went to an open-air farmer's market. Anthony bought a big old loaf of bread. On the way back to the airport, John broke off hunks of the bread for us to eat for a quick lunch before getting on the plane. Saying goodbye to M was hard, but she only had two weeks left, and then she would be back in Ohio with everyone. Her flight back to Columbus was on December 5th It arrived in the evening and John greeted her with his great smile and a bouquet of flowers. We wanted M to have the evening with John alone, so Anthony and I went to Columbus the following day. We spent a couple days there with M and Lynn. M's absolute favorite time of the year is Christmas. She came home at a good time. A joyous season.

The most fun we had was going out to buy a Christmas tree with M and Lynn. We found a little, live "Charlie Brown" tree that fit perfectly in the corner of the living room. They bought a stand and lights. It was up and decorated in no time. Also, we went grocery shopping to stock up on the foods M would be needing to follow her suggested menu. We had quality time hanging out together. M stayed home from work one week and then re-entered the normalcy of life. That takes us to the end of the journey.

M does continue to battle with ED, but she has taken HUGE strides in her recovery. In my heart, I know M (with God's help) will continue to move forward and thrive both physically and mentally. So, this is the end of the journal. Goodnight, Moon. Always, remember, Meg: You are Kind. You are Beautiful. You are Smart. You are Important.

Just a few more thoughts, before I go. Here's a snippet I found in the newspaper, which couldn't have been more fitting to M's situation:

"God's plans for you are for good. So each morning, embrace the attitude that believes, 'This problem is not going to stop me; it is going to advance me,' 'My situation may look impossible, yet God will cause me to triumph over it,' 'I may have spent years in this adverse circumstance, but God is restoring the years that were stolen,' 'My hands may be tied with this problem, however, God's hands are not tied and a solution is on its way.'"

Now, for a few more random points. Arizona, where Remuda was located, was very brown and desolate. The only thing you see are huge cacti. It became more beautiful the longer we were there. Azure blue skies, sunshine every day, no clouds. Actually, Wickenburg had a lot of green vegetation, too. It was totally different from the East: different cacti, tall and round and skinny with bursts of colors on top. The temperatures were cold in the mornings but warmed to about 70 degrees F in the day. It was never hot enough where you were uncomfortable. It's a dry heat, so you don't sweat. You see coyotes running across the plains like we see deer in Ohio. There are big spiders. There are tarantulas. Even snakes!

On the topic of Dr. N (the healing service we attended), we discovered that he did, indeed, straighten M's back and made her taller. She was measured at Remuda and she is now officially 5 feet and 9 inches, just like me!

On the topic of John, the girls at Remuda went "gaga" over him. They never got to see guys during their stay. They all said he looked like a movie star (M agrees).

About the moms of the girls, all the moms had or bordered with an ED. All of them had a deep relationship with God, too. In 2008, I had an experience that brought me very close to God. I can't remember the exact time sequence, but the light of God came into my life when M was having a dark time. He was carrying me. For about two weeks, I experience an incredible journey with God. It was an out of body experience. I know it sounds crazy. I know my family was worried about me. They thought something was wrong with me. To me, it was the most awesome experience in my life. I will never forget it. I was truly in the hand of God. I feel like God walks by my side every day of my life now. The journey culminated with me having a panic attack. Anthony and M took me to the urgent care. To this day, I can't help but wonder if the receptionist, nurses and doctor were some sort of angels. Angels here on Earth? I think so. M referred to one girl at Remuda as her angel, Christa. Christa was about 40 years old and suffered with an ED for many, many years. She was extremely close to death, but she still took time to talk to M. She encouraged M not to let ED destroy her life.

I'm not sure what God's plan is for M, but my heart says He has something special in mind. Maybe ED is making M a stronger person, more in tune to other people's struggles. She is compassionate, caring, and thoughtful. Will M be a voice to help conquer ED? She says it's becoming rampant among young women. ED is a demon. Maybe God has enlisted M to destroy him. He gave her the gift to write. He placed her on a college campus, where she was more and more women being destroyed by ED. M wants to write a book. She will write a book. She has great determination.

I hope this journal will provide some insight into a mother's struggle when her most precious child is hurt by an ED. You will make a difference in this world, Meggie. And always remember:
I love you to the moon and back.

Epilogue

February 2011

As part of my continued recovery, I decided to tell my story as part of the National Eating Disorder Awareness (NEDA) upon my return from Remuda. I learned that I needed to be honest with myself. I didn't need to hide my story any longer. Late February, I visited The Ohio State University and presented to a small group of students. Here's the personal testimony that I shared:

It started slow. I began becoming more attuned to my body and changes, having always been a late developer. My junior year of college, my suitmate confessed she had an eating disorder, my senior year of college, my best friend confessed she had been struggling with bulimia nervosa since the age of 12. I attended Ohio Wesleyan University and was a collegiate athlete, competing in varsity cross-county, indoor track and outdoor track. I noticed that all the top runners were toned, fit and wavering on the side of too thin. Could I improve if I just lost a few pounds?

The restriction started and snowballed quickly. I lost 20 pounds in a matter of months and looking back at those pictures, I looked scary. It gave me a sense of control, of power. When everything else was spinning out of control, like graduate school decisions, moving back home with my parents and losing that tight social network continually provided while in college, I could turn to my eating disorder. It was always there.

I struggled with anorexia for three years and then began turning bulimic. My body was starved, my brain was starved. I began to eat, but also began to purge. I went through ups and downs for the next three years, overexercising, binging and purging and restricting. I missed my best friend's wedding shower, another friend's bachelorette party, and had a miserable time at my oldest sister's wedding, feeling forced to eat dinner and obsessing rather than enjoying. Always a loyal and honest person, I began making up excuses to skip social functions centered on food, I became manipulative with my family, saying I already ate or going to the gym in the middle of the night to burn excess calories. I was out of control and I was no longer just hurting myself, I was hurting those that I loved.

It took a long time to realize professional, intensive treatment was necessary. I didn't think I needed help. I didn't think I was unhealthy. I didn't think I deserved food.

I hit a wall eventually though, when my marathon obsessions became unhealthy, my boyfriend became fed up with my "bad" days where I would isolate due to low self-esteem and binging and purging or simply not having the energy to go out on a date, my family was concerned and the worry and panic in their hearts wasn't fair. I was hurting those that loved me with this terrible disorder. So, I picked up the phone and I called Remuda Ranch. An inpatient facility, specializing in eating and anxiety disorders, I spend 45 days in inpatient treatment, rewiring my brain and working on perfectionistic tendencies and improving self-esteem, relying on God and growing strong both spiritually and mentally. I've been in recovering for three months now, and there are still hard days, but I can say the determination and skills I've become equipped with pull me through. My entire perspective and attitude have changed. I just want to thank you all for listening to my personal story, coming tonight shows that you care about this painful disorder and I hope all of you work to lessen the stigma......

I've had a hard time continuing to share my story, worried that people will judge my character, see me as superficial for wanting to be "thin". I remind myself that it's not about the food, it's not about being thin; it's about feeling powerless and not good enough. I still struggle by turning to food as a control factor, something that no one can take away from me. I'm not perfect, but I'm better.

That's another struggle I've seen in recovery. I want to be perfect in my eating and exercise regimens. I gave up my life for 45 days to get back to a healthy life. I'll never be perfect though; ED will always have a piece of my mind, but my soul will overpower him. Recovery has been a bumpy road with stress still culminating in days of restricting. I still pray to accept this reality, as I know persistence will lead to healthier behaviors as the years pass and positive thoughts will embody my mind.

This book has helped me regain stamina in sharing my story in the hopes that by sharing the story, the struggle and the truth, others may be more open to erasing the stigma and realizing that one in ten women have these horrific thoughts, to some degree.

June 2011

The summer after Remuda, I was able to rejoin the family vacation to Hilton Head South Carolina without solely focusing on how awful my body would look in a bathing suit. A huge step, I felt confident in my bright teal Victoria's Secret bikini, which I could fill out. The spandex material wasn't drooping on me, like two years ago, and my chest didn't look skeletal. I still went running every morning that year, and I struggled going out to eat every night, not knowing the caloric intake I was consuming at varying restaurants, but I wasn't subsiding on diet cherry coke and three life savers per day, followed by nibbling on salad at the family dinners, like just a few years ago. One year, I remember starving most the week and then sneaking back to the room only to consume three ice cream sandwiches in a row. I was so humiliated and ashamed, I went to bed. Mom and dad knew what had happened. They stayed with me that night, passed up going out to enjoy their evening while all the others went for some fresh seafood. They were always there for me. For that, I am forever in debt.

October 2011

For my 28th birthday, my mom, dad, sisters and brother-in-laws joined me for a dinner celebration at a Japanese delicacy. I remember sitting at the table, just taking it all in, celebrating the fact that I was surrounded by my family and enjoying an evening full of FOOD. I never would have thought this was possible, just one year ago. My niece, Mollie, was there, too. She was just 2 months old, innocent and sweet. I will do everything in my power to keep her away from the ED pandemic. I only hope that by the time she is an adolescent, the obsession with thinness and portrayal of unhealthy BMIs through models are obsolete.

For my gift, my mom gave me her journal that she wrote throughout my stay at Remuda, as depicted throughout this book. She wanted to have it to me as a symbol of hope and progression, one year from my departure to the scariest days of my life at inpatient treatment. Look how far I had come, I thought. My mom and dad also gave me a necklace with a moon symbol and pearl, engraved with our saying 'I love you to the moon and back,' which I wear every day. As a reminder that no matter where I am or what this life brings me, I always have love and support. We are all covered by the same moon, no matter where we are in life.

January 2012

I continue to work on my doctorate degree, slowly but surely, with hopes of becoming a college professor. Working in the college environment excites me, and I feel at home. The passion and promise imbedded in college students is contagious and I'll forever enjoy working with such individuals, in some capacity. For now, I've transitioned to working at a non-profit, planning events and fundraising to fight cancer. I left my job at the alma mater when this opportunity arose, suggested by a respectable co-worker and drawn to it because of personal battles with cancer to those who I am near and dear. I enjoy my job with two events being endurance related, raising money through running and biking. I think God wanted me to do this job for a while, recognizing that running CAN be a wonderful thing, especially when connected to a cause greater than itself.

I've learned to allow myself to indulge in French fries once in a while, and I join my co-workers to lunch every so often. For years, I restricted all day until I was ravishingly hungry. I never ate lunch, except for perhaps a piece of chocolate from a co-worker's candy jar, in hopes that it would keep my blood sugar high enough to prevent me from passing out at an important meeting of sorts. I'd run in the morning before work and in the evening after work; I'd oftentimes escape to the gym over the lunch hour to squeeze in 40-minutes on the elliptical. Now, I go for a run in the morning, for the right reasons. It awakes my muscles and fills my lungs with fresh air. I often eat breakfast afterwards. I enjoy meals with John in the evenings. He's the best cook. His support has only increased. He is still the best, and I know he always will be.

March 2012

I went out to a wine tasting with Fannie last night. We had a grand time, laughing and joking until our stomachs hurt and the whole place of ritzy folks looked at us like we were crazy. We wouldn't have it any other way. We noshed on olives, cheese and grapes and indulged in six tastings of wine. I wasn't obsessing about the calories. I was enjoying the evening. I have come so far.

We started talking about our EDs, which we often did, as we knew each other completely understood. Though I pray every day that Fannie will recover and get healthy, I'm glad we have each other as sounding boards, as support through the toughest days. She is my angel, and I hope I can be hers. We can pull each other through this.

Fannie confessed that she hadn't been doing too swell the past couple of weeks. She had been more obsessed than ever. Logically, we both know, the human body cannot sustain health without proper nutrition. We talked about how we wanted to marry and have children, bring them up together. ED cannot be a part of this.

Fannie explained that she can be kicking ass in life, getting straight As in her master's program, running 7 miles and making great money in her job, but the second she steps on the scale, if the number is not low enough (or at least, in her mind, acceptable), nothing else matters. If she is failing in all aspects of her life, but the number on the scale is low and good, she feels like a success. It seems so backwards, but I totally get that. I think many women out there totally get this. Why do we deduce our self-worth to the number on the scale, the size of our jeans and the measure of our waist? This needs to stop. This society is messed up. It has to stop.

Thank you for taking the time to read about a raw and real process of recovery from an ED. May this open your eyes to the depths of the disorder, raise awareness, and stop those who are 'on the edge' to get help before ED steals years of beautiful life. Stay tuned for a sequel; I thoroughly plan to keep on the track toward full recovery.

Look at the moon. Believe in the power of God, and no matter where you are in life, no matter what struggle you are battling, everything will be okay.

Thank you, Remuda, for saving my life. I'm certain
you'll save many others.

12001958R00109

Made in the USA
Charleston, SC
04 April 2012